My Students Taught Me How To Teach

Jim Seaman

Copyright © 2021 by Jim Seaman

All rights reserved. No part of this publication may be reproduced, distributed, or transmitted in any form or by any means, including photocopying, recording, or other electronic or mechanical methods, without the prior written permission of the publisher, except in the case brief quotations embodied in critical reviews and other noncommercial uses permitted by copyright law.

ISBN: 978-1-63945-166-1 (Paperback)
        978-1-63945-167-8 (E-book)

The views expressed in this book are solely those of the author and do not necessarily reflect the views of the publisher, and the publisher hereby disclaims any responsibility for them.

Writers' Branding
1800-608-6550
www.writersbranding.com
orders@writersbranding.com

Table of Contents

Dedication v
Introduction ix
Chapter 1 My First Year 1
Chapter 2 From High School to 2nd Grade 7
Chapter 3 My Guardian Angel 15
Chapter 4 Fortune Cookies 19
Chapter 5 My Checkbook Program 23
Chapter 6 April Fools Pranks 27
Chapter 7 The Holiday Season 31
Chapter 8 The "B" Word 37
Chapter 9 My New Backpack 41
Chapter 10 Unorthodox Classroom Solutions 45
Chapter 11 Assemblies 53
Chapter 12 Teaching Sex Education To 5th and 6th
        Graders 61
Chapter 13 U. S. Constitution Day 67
Chapter 14 Some Favorite Lessons and Projects 71
Chapter 15 Some Great Principals 77
Chapter 16 Field Trips 83
Chapter 17 T-shirts, Spirit Days and Uniforms 89
Chapter 18 Some Interesting Pictures, Posters And A
        Pencil Graveyard 95

Chapter 19 Some More Lessons and Projects 103
Chapter 20 How to Make Reading More Fun 111
Chapter 21 The Kids 117
Chapter 22 Some Sad Memories 127
Chapter 23 Poems to My Students 135
Chapter 24 Some More Crazy Stuff 149
Chapter 25 Report Cards 153
Chapter 26 Yearbook 157
Chapter 27 Secret Pal 163
Chapter 28 Walk to Math 167
Chapter 29 Professional Certification (Pro cert.) . . . 171
Chapter 30 Departmentalization and Looping My Slant:
   Popular But Wrong 175
Chapter 31 The Pencil Incident 179
Chapter 32 My Last Year 183
Chapter 33 Life as a Substitute Teacher 187
Chapter 34 Zero Tolerance 195
Chapter 35 Leave No Child Behind 199
Chapter 36 My Take 205
Chapter 36 Conclusion 217

Dedication

I would like to dedicate this book to my students. But rather as a general dedication to my students, I wanted to list each student by name. In an effort to recall names, I used grade books, class pictures, yearbooks and in some cases, my memory. Since I had no idea I would be writing a book and dedicating it to my students, it's possible I omitted some names. If any of my students come across this book and discover their name is not included, please forgive me. The names of my marketing students are not included as I was unable to find their names.

Thank you to an amazing and talented group of diverse students who taught me the meaning of dedication, the realization that students can have fun and laughter and perform at a higher level and helping me to find unique ways to become a successful and effective teacher.

Thank you:

Jacobus, Misi, Dung, Devonne, David, Tessa, Narida, James, Tom, Laura, Vinh, Catherine, Taylor, Jerome, Ricardo, Windy, Stephanie, Edgar, Bryan, Peter, Saul, Mary, Christian, Erika, Jacqueline, Lynette, Muhammad, Marilyn, Arturo, Richard, Christopher, Nicholas, Augustin, Rakso, Maninderpal, James,

Jessica, Hayley, Savendra, Lam, Oksana, Amber, Amy, Anne-Marie, Betty, Breanna, Carly, Jaki, Kristen, Kristy, Maira, Ronda, Shannon, Venise, Adan, Andy, Devin, Jamil, Jerry, Josiah, Justin, Kevin, Nathan, Thuan, Tony, Veasna, Amy, Brandi, Brandy, Dayanne, Helen, Julie, Puanani, Sabneet, Sofia, Stacey, Thuy, Vivian, Blaine, Carl, Chez, Doan, Josh, Julian, Kevin, Kyle, Nate, Paylin, Ray, Sunny, Tim, Tony, Trevor, Yahya, Tim, Payton, Sean, Justin, Abdiana, Jose, Tommy, Jimmy, Riley, Khanh, Rose, Chareece, Khoi, Micky, Peter, Adal, Hal, Amanda, Stacy, Sarah, Sandra, Jomar, Isaias, John, Jingsan, Chris, Trevor, Charmaine, Marisol, Teresa, Arie, Junior, Demarco, Ahjanae, Shelby, Carvin, Jacob, Brian, Feliciano, Valeria, Alejandro, Joseph, Veronica, Leighton, Brian, Datsima, Jady, Sina, Dale, Luis, Garrett, Conner, Jerry, Antonio, Vanisa, Rheina, Brandon, Edurado, Charlotte, Armando, Tran, Kalie, Carlos, Mohammed, Miriam, Ruth, Tony, Maria, Matthew, Luz, Francisco, Tacia, Derrick, Jason, Kelly, Lisa, Ngoc, Jason, David, Uziel, Emma, Jasmine, Gaige, Brindai, Lucus, Raquel, Victoria, Abel, Kelli, Fatima, Kurtis, Natalie, Itzel, Valery, Eric, Paige, Oscar, Mirella, Apryll, Yannah, Ibrahim, Shannon, Chance, Alex, Miguel, Rocio, Amie, Roberto, Anastasia, Miriam, Nayeli, Ellique, Ryan, Monesha, Keikilani, Dylan, Nuon, Desteni, Akyra, Jamie, Laina, Francisco, Gulled, Stephany, Trey, Dustin, Miranda, Lee Lee, Adriel, Marady, Gayle-Lynn, Kenny, Michelle, Breanna,

Juvaun, Tausaga, Cynthia, Kierre, Griselda, Brian, Johnny, Trinh, Renata, Jacob, Fatima, Yesenia, Feliti, Raymond, Phearany, Patricia, Angela, Daizah, Amy, Alyson, Alexandra, Ricardo, Bumsock, Dion, Isabelle, Alex, Meylin, Alex, Aidee, K-Lynn, Aaliyah, Terra, Tom, Kenneth, Chris, Gema, Jade, Jenny, Thai, Lucy, Harlyn, Tammy, Brendan Hahjir, Henri, Juan, Maria, Alejandra, Anessa, Makeyla, Jaquilence, Diana, Julio, Brianna, Chakravit, Erika...

And I hope you are all successful, productive and happy.

Jim Seaman

Introduction

I had thought about teaching when I was in high school. I thought about it again when I was in college, but chose to major in psychology and minor in marketing rather than pursue a degree in education. I was interested in consumer psychology which addresses the purchasing habits of shoppers and why they're attracted to specific colors, packaging, merchandising, advertising and other store presentations.

I was unable to get a job in that field, as the rejection letters seemed to all say the same thing: we only hire if you have experience. So I got a job in a bank as a management trainee and soon got fired. Not learning my lesson, I got another job in a different bank and became a two time firee. During the next 25 years, I had jobs in retailing, purchasing and sales and then became a Hickory Farms franchisee for 18 years.

After my wife and I lost our house in the Northridge, California earthquake in 1994, we moved to Seattle. After working for Sports Authority, Ross and Petco, all in store management, I knew I had to get out of retail and once again thought about teaching. With one-third of my working life still ahead of me, I knew I had to make a serious change into a field where I could help people, use my creative skills and achieve a sense of accomplishment.

I once again thought about teaching, but wasn't sure what level, what subject or what grade. Someone suggested that since I used advertising and marketing skills as an entrepreneur with my Hickory Farms store, I should think about teaching marketing. I talked to the marketing teacher at my daughter's high school and became inspired and motivated. My new career was a year and a half away, my life had a goal and I started my journey to realize this dream.

In my quest to find a college, I discovered South Seattle Community College offered a teacher certification program as part of an extension of Western Washington University out of Bellingham. After talking to an advisor, things got better than I could ever have imagined. This particular college required less credits than typical to obtain a teaching certificate in vocational education. I registered to take 2 evening classes per semester. After 3 semesters of classes, I was ready to launch my student teaching. I visited a high school on Mercer Island, talked to the marketing instructor and was accepted as her student teacher.

I was working as an assistant manager at Petco and when I told the store manager I was pursuing a college program to become a teacher, he was very accommodating with regard to my school schedule. When I started my student teaching, I was able to work nights. It was a grueling schedule for almost two years, but necessary to fulfill my dream job.

As a student teacher, I mostly observed in the beginning weeks, but soon started teaching 1-2 lessons each day. After about a month, an unforeseen event caused my responsibilities to accelerate. The regular teacher's mother became ill and she had to leave the state and take care of her for the duration of the school year. It was my good fortune that the principal agreed since I was performing at a high level and had my own business, that I would be able to teach the class as its regular instructor. Since I did not have my teaching certificate, there had to be a full time sub in the room at all times for legal reasons.

This was an amazing opportunity, as it strengthened my resume for a marketing teacher in the fall. I received my teaching certificate at the age of 53. At the end of the summer, I was hired to teach marketing at Evergreen High School, but I was unprepared for what came next.

Chapter 1

My First Year

The students walked in and took their seats for the first period. After the bell rang, I introduced myself and took attendance. Before I had a chance to tell the class a little about who I was, one of the students asked me how long I had been teaching marketing. I looked at my watch and then at the class and said, "About 5 minutes". While most teachers only had to worry about lesson plans, quizzes and tests, classroom management, grading, report cards, conferences, open house, parent phone calls, meetings and taking additional courses, a marketing instructor also had to select students to run the snack store, oversee the purchasing of food and drink items and prepare students who wanted to compete in the DECA competition. This was a class in which students are preparing to become leaders and excel in marketing, finance, fashion design, hospitality and management. There is competition at the local level, regional level, state level and national level.

As a first year teacher I was fighting with the challenging behavior of teenagers, the stress from being pulled in too many directions and wondering why our calendar system only provided 24 hours in a day. When facing a difficult schedule, many of us tend to prioritize, and for me, my number one priority was having my lessons prepared, necessary handouts copied and creative projects in place. My managers ran the snack store and I focused on the classroom.

Marketing is an elective which describes everything that happens within a service or a product from the time it is conceived until the time it is in the hands of the customer or the customer utilizes the service. This includes determining if there is a market for your product or service by using marketing research, the production, distribution to stores, pricing, merchandising, advertising, promotion, selling and financing.

Since this is an elective, I assumed the students would be eager to sign up for this class to be able to compete in the DECA competition, to learn more about a subject in which their interest had been piqued or because they had an entrepreneurial spirit they may want to pursue one day. I was not prepared for disruptions, disrespect and non-compliance of assignments from 2 to 3 students in each class. All students are required to choose one elective, and since many of the popular electives fill up, the counselors may place some of the kids in marketing who would rather not be there. I did not realize that this situation, combined with my lack of disciplinary skills from being a first year teacher, would later lead to serious problems and consequences.

Luckily, the majority of students were eager to learn this subject and exhibited amazing and creative talents in completing challenging and engaging projects. The first part of the curriculum involved educating the students in the various aspects of marketing which were mentioned earlier. With each segment, the students completed a short project. If they were learning about marketing research, they would have to prepare a survey for future customer interest in a product, give that survey to another class, tabulate the results and then determine if there is enough interest to manufacture the product.

After the students had learned all the marketing strategies, they then had to choose a service or create a new product. They also had to complete all the marketing steps, write a paper and prepare a poster or powerpoint presentation to the class. What better way to teach a subject than utilizing real life situations with hands-on learning.

The operation of the snack store was part of the marketing program. It was run by three managers and a group of responsible students who sold food and drinks. I was not aware there were students stealing cash, taking food and not charging their friends for merchandise. When large shortages were discovered through an inventory and money was taken out of an unlocked safe, the store was closed and there was an investigation by district security.

The managers, student employees and several student customers were interviewed with recorded and written documentation. I had not taken inventories on a regular basis, so much of the blame came back to me and rightfully so. Teaching 6 classes, being responsible for the operation of the store and preparing students for DECA competition finally had taken its toll on me.

I wasn't sure if security thought I was directly responsible for the theft and other losses, but the situation was a nightmare, affecting my teaching and life at home. The investigation eventually led to a confrontation at the district with the head of security, my principal, and legal representation provided to me by the teacher's union. I was extremely concerned that my teaching career would be over before I completed my first year of teaching. What also terrified me was that I would not be able to secure another teaching job in any district.

After the district meeting, it was determined that I would keep my job and the store would be closed for the rest of the year. I wasn't sure what any future repercussions might be or how this would affect my teaching for the following year.

At the end of the school year, all high schools have to estimate what their student enrollment will be for the following year. Their calculations revealed there would be approximately 150 fewer students, for various reasons, which meant there would be 6 teachers laid off. Since the core subjects and special education classes could not be touched, the only remaining direction was to eliminate most electives which included, drafting, photography, wood shop, auto shop, life skills and marketing. I did think it was interesting that the school decided to retain ceramics and weight lifting in place of life skills and marketing, but it was not my place to question which classes would be bumped.

All new teachers are usually on a non-continuing contract which must be renewed for the following year. I was very fortunate to receive my new contract before the marketing program was eliminated. Even though I would receive my contracted pay and benefits, I had no class to teach. As a result, I became a contracted substitute teacher for my second year. This meant I would be sent to any school, any subject and any grade where there was an opening for that day.

My dream of teaching marketing was gone and my job in education suddenly became fraught with unhappiness, frustration and stress. I wasn't sure what impact the stealing and closing of the snack store would have on my future teaching career. After a month my life would change, although, at that time, I had no idea it was about to go a little farther downhill before I would find myself in what we all hope to one day call, 'the perfect job'.

Chapter 2

From High School to 2nd Grade

When I started to sub in 2000, even though technology was pretty far along, it had not yet caught up to the substitute teaching system. If a sub was needed in a classroom within my school district, the teacher entered their absence in the computer, and the sub office would make calls from their sub pool to secure a substitute teacher. If a sub wasn't comfortable teaching high school students due to their size, and at times mean spirited attitude, they didn't have much of a choice in turning the assignment down. The same thing was true for a kindergarten class or the challenge of teaching to the raging hormones of a 6th grade class.

Since I had a contract, I had to work every day. Sometimes, the sub plans were incomplete or not very clear. Sometimes, I would question the fact that the plans seemed inadequate and if I were the teacher, I would teach the curriculum differently in order to hold the students interest or make it more fun. Sometimes, there were no lesson plans. Basically, subbing was stressful, not very rewarding and was not fulfilling my dream to teach.

One day I called the sub office and asked if I could request a long term assignment so I would get the feeling that it was my class and I wouldn't have to bounce around so much. My request was answered in the form of a second grade class. The transition from high school to second grade was a shock to my system. The regular teacher had been in an automobile accident and her injuries did not allow her to return for the balance of the school year.

For the next 8 months, I felt as if I was on life support, spending much of my time in the other second grade teacher's rooms asking for clarification, suggestions and assistance. I remember one day I was teaching a geometry lesson about shapes. When I came across the rhombus, I asked myself, "What the hell is a rhombus?" I tried to remember my geometry lessons when I was in elementary school, but drew a blank so I concluded it must be a newly discovered shape like an astronomer locating a new galaxy.

Even though the subject matter was new and the student ages were challenging, I did my best to make it fun for the kids and satisfy the required curriculum. But as the year continued, I felt I would not be able to complete this long term assignment. I wrestled with sticking it out versus asking to be replaced and going back to regular subbing. One day after school, I picked up the phone to be connected to the sub office to request a change. As the phone was ringing, something inside of me said, "Don't" and I immediately hung up.

That immediate change of mind was probably the single greatest decision I ever made. I didn't realize then how my life would be affected by choosing that course of action.

All teachers have the choice of what grade to teach and in the case of middle and high school, what subject to teach. I loved the second grade students. I loved teaching. I just wasn't in my comfort zone. But I decided I would be the best second grade teacher I could be for the remaining four or five months.

On photo day, in addition to the photos the kids can purchase, the teacher receives a class picture. Many teachers save these and put this collection of their memories of past students on a door or cabinet. I wish I had thought to do this, but at the time, I wasn't able to have that vision. However, I did find an 8 x 10 picture taken when I was a student in second grade and hung it in a double frame along with the picture of the second grade class I was teaching. These framed photos of me in second grade, then me teaching second grade, provided the inspiration and drive I needed to create a remarkable connection with my students.

When I was teaching the students about money I decided, in order to motivate the kids, I would put their pictures on the various bills. The lesson is taught with paper money that is a little larger than real currency, but otherwise looks exactly the same. When the students had their pictures taken for parents to buy, the teachers received a roll of their students' pictures - about the same size as those you would get from a photo booth. I didn't realize the enormity of my cutting and gluing project, but I stuck with it until all 20 students had an assortment of personal bills totaling $50.00. They bought things, made change and when they did something for which they could be rewarded, I gave them a ten dollar bill with my picture on it.

One day a student asked me what happens when someone gets arrested. It sounded as if this situation might have recently happened to a family member. I later found out it was this student's uncle. This was my awakening as an educator that there are times when you need to put part of your daily lesson on hold and teach a real life lesson. Even though there are 180 days to teach your required curriculum, most teachers would have given an abbreviated answer and continued with their current instruction. But that was not my style.

It didn't take me long to formulate what I thought would be an informative and important lesson to these 7 years olds. I gave them some background on what happens when you are arrested, including being read your rights, going to jail and your options if you can't afford an attorney. Then we had the trial. I played the role of the prosecutor, the defender, witnesses and the judge. The students understood each of my roles even though I did a lot of moving around. The class was the jury. As I was playing the role of the judge, I told the jury about "reasonable doubt" and gave other jury instructions. The students took their role seriously and at the end of the trial they voted to find the defendant not guilty. In my 13 years as a teacher, I have prepared over ten thousand different lessons, many requiring research and handouts, but not one of those was as effective and rewarding as this unprepared lesson.

On February 28, 2001 at 10:54 in the morning, Seattle was jolted by the 6.8 magnitude Nisqually earthquake. While, thankfully, no one was injured, one of the two buildings was declared unsafe. Since both buildings were necessary to accommodate all grades, we went to a half day schedule sharing the safe building. Kindergarten through 3rd grade came in the morning and grades 4 through 6th came in the afternoon.

Since my second grade class was sharing a 5th grade classroom, they did not have the inside of the desk to keep books, pencils, paper, etc. One of the other second grade teachers came up with the idea of having the students keep their supplies in a small cat litter box. All of the primary grade teachers, who were all sharing classrooms, went to every Target, K-Mart and pet store within 20 miles to purchase litter boxes for their class. I still wonder what those employees thought with this strange run on litter boxes, 25 at a time.

With only a few days left in the school year, I received a letter saying my contract was not being renewed. I understood the district did not want to pay a substitute teacher's salary along with benefits and I would have to secure a new job as a regular teacher. I was unsure what was in store for my teaching future, but I soon would receive some news that would change my life.

After the school year ended, I took a couple of days to clean and organize my room, said my good-byes to those teachers with whom I had developed special friendships and then drove out of the parking lot contemplating my potential options. I had only driven a few blocks when I heard a horn honking behind me. When I looked in the rear view mirror, I saw my principal motioning for me to pull over. He came over to my car and asked me if I wanted to be one of his 6th grade teachers for the following school year. He told me he liked my sense of humor in the classroom and that I reminded him of himself when he was a first grade teacher.

I was excited by the compliment and job offer, but I was unsure if elementary school was the direction I wanted to pursue. I was planning on seeking out openings in marketing. After I asked him if I could sleep on it and let him know the following morning, he mentioned that the way I brought fun and humor into lessons would be an asset for the older kids.

When I got home, I made some calls to see if there were any openings in marketing within a 30 mile radius of my home. There were no current openings, no future openings and if any became available, there was no guarantee I would be hired, especially considering my less than stellar performance as a marketing instructor two years earlier.

The following day, I accepted the 6th grade position. I did not realize that I was about to enter into a job that would bring personal gratification beyond my wildest dreams.

Chapter 3

My Guardian Angel

My personality, since young adulthood, has had me enjoying life, kidding around, having fun and bringing laughter into other people's lives. As a teacher, I wasn't sure if this style and approach would work in the classroom. If I did and said funny things, would the students be able to enjoy my momentary antics, but then get back on task and finish their assignments until my next outbreak of silliness? I did bring my personality into my marketing classes on a smaller scale and we had lots of fun in 2nd grade. But I wasn't sure how this would play out with puberty driven pre-teen 6th graders. I figured the answer to this question would be determined by their ability to understand that, after the fun and laughter, they had to be able to return to a level of focus and concentration that was serious.

I knew the students would play an integral role in my style of teaching. Could we laugh every day? Could we have fun every day? Could I be myself which was mostly silly and a little bit goofy? Could I introduce lessons that challenged the students to perform at a higher level? Could I make their

6th grade experience the best ever? The answers to all these questions was a resounding yes! Together, my students and I learned how to have fun learning!

With the start of my third year of teaching, I received a letter from the district stating my salary would be reduced by $10,000 since I was no longer under contract to teach marketing. When teachers were hired for vocational educational classes such as computers, drafting, photography, auto mechanics and marketing, the district knew they would have to pay them higher salaries than other teachers received in order to offer these programs to students.

In 1999, the starting salary for a teacher in my district (just outside Seattle) was $29,000.

I don't know of any teacher just starting out who works less than 60 hours per week and when you calculate the hourly wage, it is a little disconcerting. I was fortunate because I brought 18 years of marketing skills from my Hickory Farms business and as a result, received a salary of $39,000. If the regular education teachers who were making several thousand dollars less after teaching for several years were aware of this salary difference, they would be confused and upset. However, in order to offer these classes, which could possibly stir student interests in the direction of pursuing a career in these fields, it was necessary. No auto mechanic making $50,000-$70,000 per year could afford to take a job in education for $29,000.

When I found out my salary was being reduced by 25%, I wasn't sure I could afford to teach. Sometimes when you want something bad enough, you have to make sacrifices and it looked like that was going to become a reality in my life.

Then something remarkable happened. I got a call from Suzanne in the payroll department who told me she noticed my salary had taken this huge dip and wanted to make sure it was not a mistake. I told her I was no longer teaching marketing, and as a result, my pay had been reduced to that of a regular teacher. She told me she couldn't make any guarantees in getting my salary increased, but she said, "Let me look into this and see what I can do. It might take some time."

I continued to teach, be poor and wait. After 6 or 7 weeks, I received a call from Suzanne.

The first words out of her mouth were sweet and to the point: "I've got some good news for you." She apologized for taking so long to get an answer from the State of Washington Education Department. She informed me that since this situation had never occurred, there was no precedent to decide my salary issue. Therefore, it was determined that I would be "grandfathered in" which meant I would continue to receive my marketing salary even though I was no longer teaching marketing. My situation actually set a precedent if this were to occur in the future.

How is it possible to say "thank you" to someone who spotted what they thought to be a salary discrepancy on a payroll report and then took the initiative to question and rectify the situation. Suzanne not only added an additional $10,000 to my bank account, but since I continued to teach for 11 more years, she was directly responsible for me realizing an increase in pay totaling $110,000.

I knew I had to do something monumental to show my appreciation to this special angel who was watching my back. The day after her amazing phone call to me, I showed up at the district office with the largest bouquet of flowers money could buy, a huge bouquet of balloons and a hundred dollar gift certificate for stores in Southcenter Mall.

When I walked into the district office, I asked the receptionist where Suzanne's office was located. She gave me directions and as I weaved down the hallway and around the various cubicles, I could see the smiles and wondering stares on the faces of her co-workers. I'm sure there was much speculation about what was going on.

I thought about Suzanne many times during my teaching career and what she had done for me. I even called her a couple of times to say "thank you" one more time. As I write this book, I feel I need to try to reach her one last time. She left the district several years ago, but hopefully I can locate Suzanne and let her know she is a chapter in my book.

Chapter 4

Fortune Cookies

When the school year was almost over, each teacher would fill out pink (girls) and blue (boys) cards with information which would be used to determine the class rosters for the following school year. These cards would include student behavior, strong and weak subjects, work habits, if they were special ed or were on IEPs (individual learning plan) and other pertinent information that would help the teachers balance out the classes as evenly as possible.

The teachers would then get together after school to go over the cards and arrive at next year's classes. Sometimes it would get a little competitive and at times combative. If a teacher had a student's older sibling in a past year and wanted the younger sibling, or if they had a special connection with the incoming student (maybe from an after school club), there would be trades, exchanges and other forms of wheeling and dealing.

One year another 6th grade teacher wound up with a student I really wanted. I pleaded my case and offered her to any other 2 students in my class and also offered to take her lunch duty for one month. When she said no, I sweetened the pot and threw in $50.00 cash, but she still said no. Luckily, the students had no idea what went on behind closed doors!

I always wanted to be creative in just about everything I did. So when the first day of school rolled around, teachers really didn't know what would be a good seating chart. Some would let them sit anywhere for the first day or two. Others would make up a seating chart that would really be hit and miss as far as behavior problems.

I had done some fun things in the past with fortune cookies. One time before cell phones, our upstairs friend had just taken his bar exam. After several weeks, there was a number to call after 7:00 pm to find out if you passed. Since our neighbor was not going to be home that evening, and did not have access to a phone, he asked if my wife Karen and I would call and get his results. After we found out his status, we wanted to present his results in a creative way. So we went to a Chinese restaurant, brought a fortune cookie home and replaced the fortune with one of our own. We then threaded a string through it and hung it from a beam outside his front door. When he and his wife got home later that night, they opened the cookie and read the fortune which said, "You passed."

Another time, when Karen and I were in New York on vacation, we bought a container of x-rated fortune cookies.

The next time we went to our favorite Chinese restaurant in Van Nuys, California, we decided to play a trick on the owner with whom we had become friends. We took a couple of our newly purchased fortune cookies with us and when Leela brought us the cookies after completing our meal, we made the switch. I broke one in half so the fortune was visible and with a look of shock on our faces, we called Leela over to our table and showed her the x-rated fortune. She was so embarrassed! After she calmed down, she told us she was going to call the cookie company the next day to complain. She knew something was fishy when she saw the two of us laughing. We then confessed to her our purchase in New York.

So getting back to my seating chart, I decided to incorporate the fortune cookie as the directive where each student would sit. I went to the market and bought 2 boxes of fortune cookies and embarked on my project. I removed the fortunes with a tweezer and inserted new ones with a seat number on it. The white board in the front of the class had a diagram of the seating chart with the corresponding numbers. On the first day of school, I stood at the door greeting each new student and asking them to take a fortune cookie out of a bowl and remove the "fortune". I told them to then read the directions on the board to find their assigned seat.

During the next few days, I made some changes due to behavior issues, but the fortune cookies were a great way to start out my seating arrangements for the first few days of school.

Chapter 5

My Checkbook Program

I was looking to bring a real life skill into the classroom and at the same time, have it used as a discipline and reward program. Nothing came to mind quickly. In fact, nothing came to mind until the third or fourth month of the school year. Then, my "checkbook program" was created, initiated and utilized every year I taught. Not only was it successful, but it also became my teaching trademark.

The students each received a check register and "$300" in their checking account. I employed debits from their accounts for negative behavior actions such as a first, second, or third warning for behavior issues, not turning in homework, chewing gum in class, being disrespectful to another student, having to send them to another class or calling their parents. If a student was disrespectful, I would say, "Write me a check for your first warning." They wouldn't actually write me a check, but rather subtract an amount from their balance. The debit amounts were on a handout sheet to which the students had easy access.

Whenever I graded a quiz, test or project, the students would receive a dollar amount which was a deposit into their account. For example, if I gave a math quiz, I might say, "Everyone gives themselves $2.37 for each correct answer. In calculating the amount they would receive for the quiz, they had to complete a multiplication review using decimals.

When I devised this program, I became aware that some students who struggle with certain subjects, would not be receiving much money. I wanted this to be positive and not affect their self- esteem. So on everything for which they received money, I set a minimum amount that each student would receive even if they only got 1 or 2 problems correct. If I gave a 20 point spelling test and they received $1.42 for each correct word spelled and they got every word correct, they would credit their account $28.40. But if they only got 2 correct, instead of receiving $2.84, I would set an amount of 50% of the maximum amount or in this case, $14.20. No one would ever receive an amount less than 50% of the total possible amount. I also gave the lower achieving students bonus money for improvement or giving an excellent effort.

All students also had the opportunity to make money if they raised their hand to make an outstanding contribution to a class discussion. Since I strived to get the students interested in the subject and to think beyond the obvious, I always gave them high amounts for contributions.

After each 6-8 week period, I would have an auction or open up a "store". I would purchase about $75 to $100 worth of cool supplies such as gel pen sets, mechanical pencils, highlighters, decorative pencils, tie-dyed spiral notebooks, calculators, basketballs and lots of different size candy bars, licorice, etc. Usually the jumbo candy bars would go for $600-$700.

Since I obviously could not check the adding and subtracting for every entry for every student, they were on the honor system. I would eyeball their math periodically for accuracy. If their balance before an auction/store seemed too high or low, I would then check the math in more detail.

Before I rolled out the checkbook program, the class worked on several worksheet examples of debits and credits. If some students had trouble with multiplying, I had a neighboring student help them. We also had a lesson on how a banking system works when checks are written and paid.

One day, I told a student to write me a check for $21.49 for not turning in their homework.

He raised his hand and responded, "Mr. Seaman, I don't have enough money in my account to subtract that amount." I never thought about overdrafts, overdraft protection and NSF charges.

But this would happen at least once every year and as a result, the students would get an education on what happens when you write an NSF check.

Whenever I had an auction, I would hold up the item that was up for bid and tell the students, we were going to have the bidding in multiples of a certain amount such as $75.00. One student would say, "I would like to start the bidding at $75.00." Another student would raise their hand and say $150.00. The next student would have to put a little more thought into their bid before they said, "$225."

Each year, I would spend hundreds of dollars on this program for merchandise, but it was so worth it. It wasn't the perfect discipline plan, but when a student had to write a check for poor behavior, I usually got at least an hour or two before he or she repeated their negative behavior. I was always a little surprised that in 11 years of teaching 5th and 6th grade, no other teacher was interested in using this real life situation which became a daily discipline plan, a reward program and a basic math review program all in one.

Chapter 6

April Fools Pranks

During my teaching years, April Fool's Day resulted in some pretty amazing pranks on both my students and my principal. After the Seattle 6.8 earthquake in 2001, the school office was declared unsafe and a trailer housed the office personnel and principal. One day after school in March, several of the staff were at a TGIF get together and started talking about playing a prank on our principal Dave. Since April 1st was on a Monday, many of us decided we would come in on Saturday and remove all of the principal's furniture from his office. It was moved into a room located in the building that was closed due to the earthquake. The only thing that remained was his computer which sat on the floor.

The first thing our principal, Dave, did each Monday morning, was type his Newsletter to parents and staff. Since there was no desk or chair, it was funny to see Dave do the only thing he could – sit on the floor and type! All of the pictures and knick-knacks were taken from his office to classrooms, one placed in each room. With each knick-knack he recovered was a poem directing Dave to the next classroom with another personal item. We even got Dave's boss involved in our prank. When Dave walked into his office first thing in the morning, there was an email from Dave's boss leaving instructions for how he would locate his items and also the clue to get him to the first room. We borrowed a shopping cart from the Albertson's grocery store down the street so Dave would have a vehicle to pick up and store his office possessions. Deb, our office manager, followed Dave with a camcorder documenting this historical Mount View school event. When Dave entered a classroom, the students were informed of the teacher's April Fools Day prank on their principal. Dave actually got each class involved in this activity by reading them the poem and seeing if they could direct him to the next room. It took a couple of hours, but Dave recovered all his knick-knacks and was a great sport in completing this scavenger-like prank. When school was over, several teachers brought his furniture out of its hiding place and soon his office contents were returned to their original places.

It's always difficult to surpass a prank that you think could never be topped, but we still had to come up with an April Fools prank for the following year. We decided to fill up his office with balloons. I'm talking floor to ceiling, wall to wall. So on the day before April 1st, when school was over and Dave had gone home, the staff entered his office and started blowing up balloons. After his office was totally stuffed with balloons (we had to back out of his office to continue), we couldn't wait until the following morning. As soon as Dave walked into the trailer, Deb gave a coded message over the intercom so the teachers could come down to see his reaction and share in the glory of another successful prank!

Dave or "Mr. Dave" as the students called him, liked to connect with the kids. One way in which he did this was to bring his toys into the classrooms and mess with the kids as the teachers were trying to teach. Some teachers didn't appreciate his toys or the distractions they caused. Even though it could be annoying, I loved his toys and I put up with his antics. If I were the principal, I would have done the same thing. This wasn't frequent enough to be problematic and his visits were brief. But it was a great way to bond with the students.

His best toy was a plastic boxing glove which had a trigger connected to it. When you pulled the trigger, the glove would shoot forward about four or five inches. When he entered classrooms, he would walk around the room with his plastic boxing glove and press the trigger as he approached the kids. Everybody enjoyed his silliness except the teachers.

One day the staff decided to kidnap his toy. It traveled from teacher to teacher along with a polaroid camera. When they received it, they had to take it someplace off the school grounds, take a picture of it and write a note about its trip.

One teacher took it to a University of Washington Husky college football game and took a picture of it with one of the players. I took it to a Sports Authority store and laid it next to real boxing gloves with a note on the picture that said, "A reunion with my family." We then put the picture we had taken in Dave's mailbox and passed the glove and camera on to another teacher to keep this going for several weeks.

Our staff was beyond dedicated and gave more to their profession than any group of people I have ever encountered. Many stayed after school to tutor students without pay. Many worked until 6:00 and even 7:00 in the evening. Many came in on the weekends. And most took work home every night. But, in addition to their work ethics, they were unselfish in going out of their way to help each other and support our principal.

Chapter 7

The Holiday Season

The students were always eager for Christmas break. No alarm clocks, maybe some traveling, staying up late, gifts under the tree, no lessons, seeing relatives and friends and living the life! I believe that students need a break, but many teachers feel when you lose the continuity of teaching, the students will lose the momentum and they will need lots of review when they get back. But my belief was, never mind the students, I need a break! The pace for a dedicated teacher can be extremely exhausting and we all needed time off to recharge our batteries.

Most teachers in elementary school give their students a Holiday packet which includes reading, math review, writing and maybe other curriculum. Since my wife is an artist, she would always draw a picture of Santa on my packet cover page doing something funny. But she would use my school photo in place of Santa's face. This way, the kids would remember me even if they weren't in school.

One year, I decided instead of handing out the packet at the end of the last day before the Holiday break, I would present their packet in a more impactful way. I placed the packets in one box wrapped with Christmas paper. Earlier, I had found out that the assistant librarian's brother was a driver for UPS. She talked to him and he agreed to come to my classroom right after he completed his route which was before school ended.

Around 2:30, this uniformed UPS guy walked into my room with my wrapped box. As he entered the classroom, he said in a loud voice that he had a parcel for Mr. Seaman's class. The kids immediately jumped out of their seats and ran to greet him at the door. They were all thinking the same thing: Christmas treats for the class. I told them to calm down and I would pick one student to open the box. As Lisa started to unwrap the box, the students formed a circle around her, some even standing on chairs to get a better view of what they thought to be candy or some other Christmas gift. As the packets came out of the box, I said, "Oh look, Santa had your Holiday homework packets sent from the North Pole." For a moment, I thought the groans and grumbling might lead to mutiny. But the kids knew it was all in fun and I'm sure when they got home later that day and their parents asked if there was homework during the Holiday break they at least had a great story to tell.

I have to thank another teacher, Jerry, for giving me the idea of wrapping up the packets. But I always enjoy the challenge of taking an idea to a higher level. My UPS driver was a great addition to an already inspired idea by Jerry.

Most teachers have their students work on an art or craft project they can take home on the last day before the Holiday break. One year, as I was browsing a magazine, I saw a pasta Christmas tree that seemed unique. It was made with an assortment of different shaped pasta, glued on a heavy poster board that was rolled into a cone that stood about 12 inches high. Some students glued their pasta on with a different pasta type in each row. Others used the method of random gluing. Each year some even employed a ribbon effect around the tree. It was then spray painted either green, white or green with white splatters that made it appear as if it were snowing. And lastly it was sprinkled with glitter.

I would spray paint them outside and bring them inside to dry overnight. My first year was a learning experience. When I walked into my room the next morning, the fumes were so strong, I thought the students would get high and I would be arrested for students learning under the influence of paint fumes. Since our room was upstairs I was able to keep the windows open a few inches in subsequent years. If any teacher cares to duplicate this art project, be aware it takes several days to complete

The kids really enjoyed creating their trees and it became one of my signature projects. Sometimes when I ran into students many years later, they would tell me they still had their pasta tree which came out every Christmas as a tree topper or a table centerpiece.

About 10 days before the Holiday break, I had the kids cut, decorate and sign a Christmas stocking which I hung below cabinet doors. One very effective method of teaching that I employed was reviewing prior material, especially in math. For this project, I typed 12 questions, cut them into strips and put them in the student's stockings. Each day they would pull out a question, write the answer and bring it to me to check. This review enabled the students to recall important facts and solve problems while also receiving money into their checking account.

On the last day before break, I put Christmas themed pencils and wrapped Christmas candy in their stockings to take home, along with the pasta trees.

Many of you have possibly been to a Christmas party where gifts are exchanged and can be 'stolen' from you. Each year, our staff had a party before the Holiday two-week break, including this type of gift exchange. If you're not familiar with how this works, everyone brings a gift (at a set price point) and they are placed in a pile on the floor. Each person draws a number out of a hat to determine the order for choosing gifts. When it is your turn, you can either choose a wrapped gift from the pile and open it or steal a gift from anyone who has already chosen and opened their gift. A gift can be stolen up to three times.

Someone had chosen a gift which turned out to be a foot tall Santa that played *Here Comes Santa Claus* when you pushed a button. But what made this Santa unique is that he would fart throughout the song. When someone chose this gift, I was hoping to steal it, but by the time it was my turn to choose a gift, I was unable to take it away since there had already been three steals.

This was an item that absolutely had to be in my room. After the completion of the gift exchange, I went up to Marjean and offered her $20.00 for the farting Santa. She agreed to the sale and I got my Santa. The kids loved it, especially the ending of the song, which included a very long, loud and juicy fart.

A couple of years later, Santa was stolen from my room. At first I thought it was a student, which saddened me, but a few days later I received a ransom note. It said to bring a bag of large unmarked bills to the library at 6:00 p.m. and if I did not comply, I would start receiving body parts in the mail. Obviously, I did not comply and I could only hope that my kidnapped Santa would not be harmed. I was pretty sure the thief was my principal, but could not prove it. Luckily, I did not get any arms or legs in the mail. As the school year moved on, there were no more threatening ransom notes. I wasn't sure if I would ever see Santa again.

On the last day of school, we had a party at a teacher's house. When I walked into the backyard, I noticed a picnic table with chips, dips, fruit, desserts and my farting Santa as a centerpiece! As I glanced around and spotted the principal, the broad smile on his face was an absolute admission of guilt.

Chapter 8

The "B" Word

Sometimes teaching can get very frustrating, stressful and unpredictable. We have certain professional standards of behavior to follow. But once in a while we slip into the world of being human where words are uttered or even screamed that are not appropriate for children.

I've heard tales from teaching colleagues who have yelled four letter words, not at specific students, but rather at the class as a whole. The second the word bounces off your vocal cords, there is one immediate thought that comes to mind. Is someone in the class going to tell mom or dad when they get home from school and are you going to find yourself sitting in the principal's office the next day? A teacher friend told me there were days when he would have given a thousand dollars to be able to say to his class: "shut the f---- up" and not get in trouble for it!

I have always been more calculating. Rather than using the two or three words that could get you in trouble, my swear word of choice was "crap". As I sensed my level of control reaching its limits, I was somehow able to refrain from shouting an obscenity I would later regret. I would take about 2 or 3 seconds to evaluate the situation and plan my verbal swear word attack. It usually was, "Knock that crap off! Now!" The next five seconds revealed shock on their faces, silence from their lips and the knowledge that you were going to get great behavior for the next 30 minutes. Usually.

There was one situation where I did cross the line. The class was walking across the field from our portable to the library. One student was loud, obnoxious and out of control. I told him 2 or 3 times to settle down. When he continued his unacceptable behavior, I lost it and told him to stop being such a bitch. Not only was it personal, but it wasn't even an appropriate swear word.

The next day I told some teachers what I had said and they all told me the same thing: I had to tell the principal. I wasn't sure what the first words out of my mouth were "Are you crazy?" or "Why in the world would I do that?" But they all had the same answer, I finally decided made sense. They said it would be important that Dave did not get blindsided if he got a call from the parent. I was really nervous, but I sucked it up and walked into his office later that day.

I racked my brain for a way to tell Dave that would sound less offensive, but there really wasn't any way to diminish the impact of my actions. I sat down and told him what had happened up to the time of my swearing. So far so good. But then I said the part about "stop being such a bitch". He then raised his voice to a slight scream in a barely recognizable octave and said, "You said WHAT!" I repeated it. He repeated his first comment. It seemed like there was silence for a few hours, but after a few seconds, he told me I had to call his mother and tell her what I told her son and apologize. I thought I was nervous talking to the principal, but that suddenly became the easy part. I told Dave I would call her that night.

After dinner, I planned my strategy. It was a good plan and I was hoping it would take some of the sting away. When she answered the phone, I first asked her if her son had told her what I said to him the prior day. She answered, "No". I told her I was having a terrible time, things hadn't gone well during the day and I wasn't feeling well. I then told her what her son had done. I tried not to stutter when I then told her that I had said: "Tommy, stop being such a bitch!" I feared what her reply would be, but I wasn't prepared for the response. She said, "Well, he IS a bitch". She probably heard my sigh of relief as my breathing started to return to normal.

I replied, "Even so, I should not have said that and I want to apologize to you." I also told her I had already apologized to her son. Thankfully, what could have been a volatile situation turned out to be a minor incident with a lesson to be learned: don't ever make it personal. The next day I told

Dave what mom had said and he was as relieved as I was. I should add, I still use the word "crap" when I am desperate for 30 minutes of good behavior.

Chapter 9

My New Backpack

My wife and I were looking to purchase a southwest tribal blanket. Our research of what would be our best stores to shop for this item, brought us to Pendleton's in downtown Seattle.

Their selection of designs was abundant and beautiful, but the prices were beyond our price range. As we walked around the store, we fell in love with just about everything, but left with nothing. I did see a backpack with a southwest Indian design for $135.00 that I had to one day own. It just wasn't going to be that day.

A few weeks after my futile shopping trip, Dave sent an email to all teachers that he wanted to meet with us after school in the lunch room for just a few minutes. When he walked in, he was holding about 25 white large envelopes. What happened next, was one of the most unexpected and amazing things that could happen to anyone in their workplace. It certainly was for me.

Dave told us that a man had come into the office and given sealed envelopes to Deb, our office manager, requesting she deliver them to our principal. Accompanying the envelopes was a letter that this mystery person had written and directed Dave to read to his teachers.

The letter told us that this man worked at Boeing and each year he received a bonus that he wanted to give back, in some way, to his community. His gift to the recipients varied each year and this year he had chosen the classroom teachers at Mount View Elementary school. His letter said he did not have any children in our school nor did he have any connection to it. But he was in awe of the dedication we all gave to our students.

It appeared he had done some research about our kids and the struggles many were facing as they were growing up. His research included knowing the names of each teacher. He also asked that each of us put this gift toward something that would be a reminder of our tireless contributions to children. He made a point that he would prefer we use it in a personal manner or toward classroom essentials rather than using it to pay bills or for grocery shopping.

Dave then handed out the envelopes, each with our name on it. All 25 teachers found a new $100.00 bill inside. For days we speculated who this might have been, but we kept coming back to his statement saying he had no connection to our school. This unusual gesture put an awful lot of warmth in our hearts that day, not only for the gift, but also for the respect and appreciation he had for the job we do. He knew that for us it's much more than a job.

    I wanted to do something really special with my gift. It didn't take long to remember my backpack at Pendleton's. When I bought it, I knew the papers to grade, the assignments to plan and other school related work that I piled in it and brought home, would remind me of this special individual and his special request for the duration of my teaching career. Now in retirement, I still use the backpack and remember his amazing generosity and kindness. Perhaps one day he'll read this book and know how much his gifts meant to us all.

Chapter 10

Unorthodox Classroom Solutions

Over the years, I did some interesting, funny and unique things in my classroom. One of my favorites was during my third year teaching. It was a difficult class at times and I needed to introduce a strategy that would have an impact on my 6th graders to be more respectful to their peers and their teacher. As I was searching for the perfect answer, I asked myself what I could do to get my kids to stop acting like kindergartners. I then realized I had my solution.

If they were going to act like kindergartners, then they would sit in kindergarten chairs. I knew there were more than enough chairs kept in a storage room so I set off on my plan. I came in at 6:30 the next morning, got the key and a hand truck from the custodian and went to work. With the hand truck, I was able to wheel about 5-6 chairs per trip. I had to travel across a field so this was a time consuming ordeal. I put the student's regular chairs around the perimeter of the room and set the little chairs facing into the large desks.

I had a hall of fame moment when the kids walked into the classroom and could not assimilate what had just happened to their chairs. I told the class to please come in and take a seat in their replacement chairs. I said, "If you are going to act like kindergartner children, then you are going to sit in kindergartner chairs." I went on to explain they could earn their regular chairs back with good behavior for a few hours. As each student demonstrated better behavior, they were then able to trade chairs.

I had written a poem on a large poster, which was taped on the white board in front of the class. It read:

When you're disruptive, best beware –
Or you'll be sitting in the "kiddie chair".
If you behave and do not slack
The comfy chair will soon be back.

This was a tremendous amount of work on my part since I also had to return the chairs. But one of my favorite things to do is take a creative and unique idea and implement it, whether it is a teaching lesson or a discipline action. Usually it sends a more powerful and impactful message and eliminates the necessity of continuous verbal reminders.

Even though students are supposed to bring 2 dozen pencils or several mechanical pencils (with extra lead) to school, it appears they are always in need of one. If a student could not afford to purchase pencils, I would give them a dozen to start with. Knowing this, each year I would buy about 600 pencils, on sale at Staples for one cent each, to have for these moments. Year after year I would still run out. I knew this had to change, so I implemented a new vocabulary word –collateral.

When a student said they needed a pencil, I told them to come up to my desk. When they approached me, I asked them for a shoe. When it was time for lunch or recess, I told them: I get my pencil back – you'll get your shoe back. The first time this happened in each class, I told them this will guarantee I get all my pencils back. Frequently they would walk back to their desk without completing our exchange and amazingly find one of their own pencils! Most of the time, they removed one of their shoes and they received a pencil. I did this for 7-8 years and never lost another pencil.

There are many ways that teachers get their classes to quiet down. Some count backwards from 5. Others use a bell or a chime. Some use a rain stick. And on and on. I used a flushing toilet. Yes, you read that right.

One weekend, while cleaning my garage, I stumbled upon the perfect attention-getter for my classroom – a one foot high plastic toilet bank. It flushed the coin down when you hit the handle. Though I didn't have a need for accumulated coins, the flush handle not only worked just fine without the coins, it actually made an amazingly realistic flushing sound. Sitting on my desk, it was handy to bring the class to a stand-still when things got a little rowdy. Unlike the bell, etc, this method never failed to produce first laughter, then compliance.

One day, some girls from another 6th grade class came into my room during recess. They were hovering around the plastic toilet and started talking and giggling. I couldn't hear what they were saying, but they left when the bell rang. They returned after school and again gathered around the toilet. I was busy with something else and did not notice them fumbling with the toilet. After a few minutes, they called me over and showed me what they had done. I noticed rolled up tissue that was inside an open paper clip which acted as a spool holder. The clip then attached to the toilet. After some high fives, laughter and compliments for their ingenious idea, my toilet was now complete with this critical missing accompaniment.

Another time, while shopping at Staples, I noticed a red button that said *easy* on it. I pressed it and it said, "*That was easy*". I immediately knew there was a place in my classroom for this! The first time I used it was right after I had taught a math lesson. I walked over to my desk and pressed the button. Everyone got a good laugh and I continued to use the button on a regular basis after many teaching lessons (but only on lessons in which the entire class understood the work).

The button and the toilet were a couple of examples of things I used that served a purpose and at the same time brought some fun and laughter into the classroom.

Some years, teachers wind up with classes that are special in their learning abilities and behavior. Other years, you might have classes that are typical in learning and behavior. And occasionally, you will have classes that are challenging and disruptive. Every class is going to have at least a few students who make it difficult for the rest of the class to learn, due to constant disruptions. But a good teacher will learn how to cope with various strategies including consequences and calls to parents.

Sometimes, though, nothing seems to work and you feel that the rest of the class is being hindered. One year, I found myself in this situation. Several months into the school year, I knew I had to have a more creative discipline plan. I had 7 students who consistently were disrespectful and had a huge negative impact on the rest of the class.

I came up with what I thought was a brilliant plan. I strategically positioned their desks around the perimeter of the room equally spaced apart from each other and facing the wall. When I was teaching a lesson, they turned around so they could see my notes on the white board, overhead projections on the screen and any other information that was visual. After my lesson, they had to turn their chairs around to face the wall and complete the assignment.

This turned out to be extremely effective. Their behavior improved, the rest of the class was able to focus better and I was proud of myself for this innovative plan. Then one day, the principal called me into his office and asked me if I had turned some of the desks to the wall. I told him yes and explained why I chose that course of action. He told me he had received a call from a parent who found my plan offensive and insisted the student be returned to sitting with the rest of the class.

The principal said this method was "old school" and I could not do it. I asked him what that meant and he replied that this type of action was done in the past, but now there were better ways to deal with behavior problems. I told him I had tried everything I could think of and since implementing this seating arrangement, the class was on task and their work improved. He still said no, so back to the drawing board I went. I couldn't come up with any new great plan, so I called parents when necessary and frequently took away privileges.

The most effective discipline plan I came up with did not happen until my last year of teaching, but it was brilliant and powerful. Years before, if a student had several warnings during the day, I would call a parent at work or home and inform them their son or daughter was out of control. Not only did the student's behavior improve, but it sent a strong message to the rest of the class who overheard the conversation.

My last year, I came up with the idea of having the student make a call to their parents during class. They had a script to read which said, "Mom, this is Johnny and I wanted to tell you that my behavior has been so bad today, the other 28 students in the class are not able to learn anything. I think I should have a consequence where you _____ (this was determined by the student and myself). Mr. Seaman would like to talk to you. Hi, this is Mr. Seaman and I wanted to see if you have any questions. How about I give you a call in a week and let you know if Johnny's behavior has improved so he can get his privileges back."

I never had a parent who was not in total agreement. Johnny's behavior always improved and his conversation reverberated in the minds of every student in the room. What better way to have a student take responsibility for his behavior.

Most teachers have a "buddy teacher", who is usually from the same grade. When a student has received several warnings, they will be sent to that room for 15-20 minutes. Sometimes the student needs to be somewhere else to reflect on their behavior and think about what they need to do to improve their attitude. In some cases, they fill out a reflection form or they may work on current assignments. This can be a powerful plan, but I decided to use it in a manner which took it to the next level.

I would ask the student if they had a sibling in a kindergarten, 1st grade or 2nd grade class. If so, I would send him or her to that class with a note to the teacher asking if they could do the work currently being taught in that class for 30 minutes. When the younger sibling got home from school, they would undoubtedly rat out their older brother or sister.

While all of the above strategies were unorthodox, I found them to be more effective than the traditional methods and in many cases, the entire class was impacted by the realization that disruptive behavior could get them in the same mortifying situation!

Chapter 11

Assemblies

Shortly after Mr. Obama had been elected our first black President my wife, Karen, surprised me. She said we had a guest and he was in the living room. When I walked in, there was President Obama, (or more accurately, a 6 foot cutout of him). I wasn't sure what I should do with Mr. Obama, but after we had a few dinners together and watched some of our favorite T.V. shows with him, he was dismissed to live in the garage. I wasn't sure if he would ever resurface, but you never know if you might sometimes need an Obama cutout.

President's Day was approaching and the teachers got an email saying there was going to be an assembly. We were encouraged to have our class participate in some manner. About half the classes participated by singing songs, reciting poems and reading about some specific President. I thought about President Obama who was living in the garage of my "white house" and tried to come up with an idea of how I could incorporate him into the assembly.

Remembering my philosophy of "Think Big", I came up with the brilliant idea of having my class perform a skit.

I wrote an amazing script for a skit and read it to the class. The students who wanted to perform signed up for the part of their choice. Cardboard Obama was on stage with Juan who was standing behind him with a microphone. A few feet away were two secret service agents on each side of the President. On the side of the stage were Mr. Obama's two children and his wife Michele. And spread out in the first few rows of the cafeteria floor was a group of my students playing the part of reporters. A microphone was passed around as they asked their questions to President Obama.

Following is the skit, which was a huge hit:
Julio: Hello, my name is Julio. Good morning everyone. Today we are very lucky to have a special guest speak to us at our assembly. Please welcome President and Mrs. Obama and their family to Mount View.
Alyson: President Obama, what kind of student were you when you were in elementary school?
Obama: I was kind of average, but one day I decided it was very important to study hard, pay attention in class and always do my best. You never know, one day I might even be elected President. Oh wait, I was!!!
Angela: President Obama, were you ever bullied when you were in school?

Obama: I was bullied a lot in elementary school because of my large ears. Although I was usually able to get a head start and outrun the bullies, because I could always hear them coming.

Gema: Did you ever fight the kids that bullied you?

Obama: No, never! That would be a really bad decision. I would always walk away. And now I'm President and they're not. So there!

Jackie: What were your favorite subjects in elementary school?

Obama: I wasn't very good in math, but I loved the challenge of word problems. I always did my math homework, so I got better and soon math was my favorite subject. Good thing, since I have to balance the budget!

Aidee: President Obama, if you could send your daughter to any school, which would you choose?

Obama: Well, I've heard really good things about Mount View. I know they have the best teachers and the kids are really nice and friendly. I would send them there if the drive from the White House didn't take four days.

Diana: This question is for Mrs. Obama. What is it like living with the President?

Mrs. Obama: Well, when he's not talking to Presidents from other countries or signing bills into law, he's a regular guy. He throws his clothes on the floor, never cleans the bathroom and sometimes falls asleep on the couch.

Aaliyah: Mr. President, did you always do your homework?

Obama: Yes, that's how I got to be smarter. And I always turned it in on time. I even still have homework in my job as President. If I don't do it I get a bad grade and I won't be re-elected.

Terra: Mr. President, what was your favorite writing assignment?

Obama: My favorite writing assignment was when I had to write a story called: "What would you do if you were President"? I still take it out and look it over once in a while to make sure I'm doing it right!

Patricia: What did you write about?

Obama: I wrote that I would always be fair to everybody, I would help people, I would try to bring everyone together and that Michele wouldn't catch me playing video games.

Brianna (Sasha, interrupting)**:** Daddy, Daddy! Can Malia and I have a sleepover at the White House?

Obama: Did you finish your homework?

Amy (Malia): Yes, we're both done!

Obama: Then yes, you may have a sleepover. But not in the Lincoln Bedroom!

Erika: Mr. President, is your job hard?

Obama: Yes, it is very hard, but because I stayed in school, went to college and laughed at Mr. Seaman's jokes, I can be successful at anything I do. And I want to leave all you boys and girls with this thought: So can all of you!!!!! Thank you for allowing me to come to Mount View and talk to you.

Maria: Hi, my name is Maria. I would like to introduce the cast of characters to you. Our secret service agents were: Chackravit, Chris, Michael and Victor. Sasha was played by Brianna and Malia was played by Amy. The reporters were played by: Patricia, Gema, Aaliyah, Aidee, Angela, Erika, Diana, Terra, Jackie and Alyson. Mrs. Obama was played by Anessa. And President Obama played by himself with help from Juan.

It was very gratifying as a teacher to have seen my students rehearse and then pull off a skit in front of the entire school.

The students attend 3 specialists each week. P.E., Music and Library, but I think it's a shame there is no drama or art. It seems to me it would have been rewarding to have music, drama and art in 3 month rotations.

After I retired from teaching, I became a substitute teacher. There are many stories I have to tell about that subject, but those will appear in a later chapter. As a sub, I got a call from my old school, Mount View, asking me if I would MC a spelling bee for the school. It sounded like fun, so I happily agreed. I wanted to do something that was preliminary to the actual bee. Something that would involve teachers and some very very long words.

This was an assembly for the entire school. There were winners determined in each class from earlier trials and they were all sitting on the stage. After I was introduced, I told the audience which included many of the parents that we were first going to have a short spelling bee from teacher volunteers. I had spent several hours researching actual words that would be impossible to spell, but the volunteers had no knowledge of my research.

After my introduction, several teachers raised their hands to show off their spelling skills, including the principal. I chose 3, the first one being the principal. She came up on stage. Standing in front of her were two students holding a 4-foot strip of cardboard on which the first word appeared. The audience of kids and teachers immediately broke into loud laughter. The first word was 45 letters long and was pneumonoultramicroscopicsilicovolcanoconiosis which means *a lung disease caused by breathing in dust from a volcano*. When the audience saw this word, they began to suspect that this was not your typical spelling bee and that a typical moderator had not been chosen to emcee the contest. The principal got the first 7-8 letters right, before the vocal reactions from the audience told her to take her seat.

The next participant was a new teacher who did not know how I operated when he volunteered. His word was 30 letters long and was hippopotomonstrosesquipedalian, which meant *pertaining to a long word*. I was shocked when he came very close to getting it right, but he too, had to take his seat.

The third word was floccinaucinihilipilification, which meant *something that is thought to not be worth anything*. Another unsuccessful attempt. I then gave the audience a short education about the longest word in English which was 1,185 letters and was the name of a chemical. It was in the Guinness Book of Records, but was taken out because it was never used.

At this point, I introduced the school librarian, who would be the moderator for the actual spelling bee. There were two things that were pretty amazing about this spelling contest. The words were the same no matter what grade the student was in. As students started missing words and had to take their seat on stage, a first grader made it through several rounds. The older kids would miss and he would continue on. He immediately became the crowd favorite and after correctly spelling a word, the applause and cheering was so loud, you would have thought you were in a football stadium. He eventually missed a word, but he outlasted about half of the higher grade winners. It was especially rewarding for me that his mother was in the audience.

The second amazing thing was the winner, who as a third grader, advanced to the regional level. He was also the Mount View winner the following year as a 4th grader.

Another happy assembly time for me was when I had a mic and went into the audience of kids sitting on the floor. I squeezed through the lines of seated students, chose one and asked them what their name was. I proceeded to have a conversation of questions about unusual and silly topics.

A typical conversation with a student went something like this: "Hi, what's your name? What grade are you in? Who is your teacher? So tell me, what do you do when you get home from school? Do you have a girlfriend? No you don't. Is there a girl in your class who you might like to be your girlfriend? Do you think she knows that you like her? Maybe you should tell her right now that you like her. If you were older, where would you take her on a date? How old do you have to be before you ask a girl out on a date? Well it was great talking to you. If you decide to marry this girl will you invite me to the wedding? See ya later. I then moved on to other students, mostly younger. By this time, many were raising their hands to be interviewed by me. All of my questions were off the top of my head and I varied my routine with each student. I did this for only two assemblies, but wish I had requested it be a regular part of every assembly. For those of you that go way back, I felt just like Art Linkletter.

These unpredictable and impromptu moments were received so well by all the students and staff and for myself, it was one of the most fun times of my entire life.

Chapter 12

Teaching Sex Education To 5th and 6th Graders

I reached into the slotted shoebox where the students dropped their anonymous questions. I had been doing this for many years and actually looked forward to answering them. The first question I pulled out asked: *What are sex toys?* I was hoping for a less loaded first question – maybe something like: *how does a woman have twins* or *how long does a period last?* Each year I tell my students I will answer any question as long as it is legitimate and not personal. So I did answer the question about sex toys. And why sex feels good? And what is oral sex? Eventually I learned how to do this without the eye twitch. I gave each student 3-4 index cards, with another 100 or so next to the shoebox on the back table. During the daily discussion, the students walk back to the table and drop their questions into the box while I wonder what is coming next.

As I grabbed a handful of questions, I read them first to myself, knowing I only have a few seconds in which to formulate my answer. Some of the more challenging questions require that I place them at the back end of the pile I am holding, hoping the bell rings before the question reappears to the top of the stack. It's always good to have additional time to answer questions like: *why do they have flavored condoms?* Or *how do lesbians have sex?*

Some of the questions are thoughtful and mature such as: *When they have sex do they ask each other who is going to start it?* Or *can a guy have menopause?*

Others can be a little "far out" and hilarious such as: *If someone had a penis and a vagina could they have sex with themselves?* Or *can ghosts have sex?*

Others could only come from the curious and unpredictable minds of pre-teens such as: *If someone farts when they are having sex what happens?* Or *what happens if the boy and girl are having sex and the boy pees in the girl's vagina?* And still others are questions you wonder how they even knew to ask such as: *why do men donate sperm to a sperm bank?*

The shoe box enables the students to ask questions without the embarrassment of having to raise their hands. It also encourages greater participation from the entire class. While the shoebox creates anonymity, there are always some students who have no inhibitions. These students frequently raise their hands to ask questions that turn many of the boys' and girls' faces bright red.

Sometimes the questions cause a little too much class participation. On one occasion, I read a question from the shoebox which asked, *"Why does the woman make noises during sex?"*

I wasn't sure what I was going to say, but before I had a chance to mull it over, one of the boys began a remarkably realistic impression of the woman's sounds. I thought I was watching Meg Ryan in the New York deli scene from *When Harry Met Sally.* I'm not sure who was laughing harder, the students or their teacher.

You come to expect the unexpected, appreciate the curiosity of the students and respect the level of maturity that most students demonstrate with this difficult subject matter. Many years ago, I had a question that asked, can a boy bleed from his penis? When I first read it, I wasn't sure why it was being asked, but I quickly realized that this 11 year old student was wondering, since a girl bleeds during her period, does the same thing happen to a boy? I was struck by the logic of this question and assured the class this does not happen.

We always require the students to use correct vocabulary, rather than slang when writing their questions or expressing them orally. But sometimes they don't adhere to this request – like a 6th grader who wrote, *"What does it mean when the girl is playing with a guy's joystick?"*

One year, a 6th grade student wrote the following question: *Why does it hurt when you're getting the baby out of China?* When I read this question, I didn't know what the student meant by getting the baby out of China. The student was willing to clarify her answer by replying out loud that it was too embarrassing to say or write the word vagina, so she preferred to call it China.

The school district in which I taught is so concerned about the nature of this subject matter, they require that all 4th, 5th and 6th grade teachers attend a workshop at the district to prepare them to teach this material. While this subject can be embarrassing and difficult for many students to learn, it is also difficult for many teachers to discuss with their class. In fact, most instructors rush through this curriculum in 3-4 days. Because of the importance of the material such as teen pregnancy and STD's, I usually spend about 2 weeks if not more.

In teaching this curriculum to my students, I personally am facing an even more embarrassing task since my last name is Seaman. In order to eliminate the giggles and laughter when I talk about semen, I use the following strategy: I write my last name Seaman on the board with its definition, a sailor or your teacher's last name I then write the word semen on the board with its definition, a fluid that carries sperm. I tell my students they now know the difference between the two words and I will give them 20 seconds to get all the giggles and laughing out of their system which will then be followed by mature behavior during the remainder of this curriculum. This approach has worked for me every year!

The school district also sends a letter home to inform parents this material is about to be taught and if they have any concerns or hesitations, they must attend a meeting either at the district or school to review the material. This consists of a grade level brochure and 2 videos, one which discusses what happens when girls get their period and the other which discusses erections and wet dreams. When parents who express concerns see the kid in an appropriate way in which the material is presented, they most always give their consent. In over 11 years of teaching this subject, I have had only one parent object to having their child present during this curriculum.

Rather than teaching sex education to the entire class, many teachers prefer to separate the boys from the girls. If there is a male teacher, he will teach the boys, while a female teacher or nurse will teach the girls. I have tried it both ways and prefer to teach my 5th and 6th graders as a coed class. By the second or third day, the students are more comfortable with this arrangement. Many even stop writing their questions on paper and raise their hands. Frequently one answer will lead to other questions asked by both genders and a mature discussion develops.

It is gratifying to see the barriers removed and have a girl ask a question directed to the male's body, such as *what is a wet dream* or a boy ask a question directed to the female's body such as, *what happens to the egg if the sperm doesn't go into it*.

Some of the questions can be personal such as: *what happens if you marry a person and they are nice and then they turn mean?* Or *what happens if you don't want to share a bed and your husband wants to share a bed?* Usually when I see questions like this, I mention at the end of the teaching session that anyone can talk to the school counselor or myself if they have concerns over any of the material we discussed or have more questions.

If any readers are interested in seeing 335 questions asked by 4th, 5th and 6th grade students and answered by their teachers, checkout <u>Where Does The Trombone Go?</u> *The Sex Ed Questions You Wouldn't Believe Kids Ask?* Available through Amazon but may be cheaper through Writers Branding. Please check www.writersbranding.com. This is a book, a 4th grade teacher and I just published.

Chapter 13

U. S. Constitution Day

One year after the first week of school, the assistant principal sent an email to the teachers requesting that they teach a lesson on September 17th, which is U. S. Constitution Day, about democracy and our Constitution. Some chose to talk about what is in the document, others showed a cartoon about it and others found some activities online.

There had been a lot in the news about enemy combatants and suspected terrorists being arrested and held in jail in Guantanamo Bay which was a military prison for extraordinarily dangerous people. They would be interrogated and prosecuted for war crimes. The one thing that made me question the fairness of this strategy, was the fact that the prisoners could be held indefinitely without even receiving a trial. Since the 6th amendment to our U. S. Constitution says everyone is guaranteed the right to a speedy trial, I was concerned about the rights of prisoners, even if they were thought to be probable terrorists. There was also the possibility they might not be terrorists.

I now had my lesson for Constitution Day. I gave the students a handout which told them that our Constitution is a document that is supposed to guarantee all Americans certain liberties and protections. They then read about an American citizen by the name of Ali Saleh Kahlah alMarri. I told them after they had read my handout about al-Marri they were to write a paper expressing their feelings about whether our Constitution really guarantees its citizens freedoms and protections or not. They would need to take a stand and argue their position.

They learned that al-Marri was a legal U.S. resident living in Illinois after coming to America from Qatar with his wife and 5 children. He was attending Bradley University to receive his master's degree. In 2001, he was arrested and charged with credit card fraud and other criminal offenses. He proclaimed his innocence and just before he was to go to trial, President Bush had him declared an "enemy combatant" and he was transferred to a Navy jail in South Carolina.

An enemy combatant is someone who the United States believes is connected with a terrorist group. Even if innocent, "enemy combatants" could be held in prison indefinitely if our Government feels they might have valuable information. They can lose all their legal protections that typical prisoners receive.

While in jail, al-Marri was subjected to torture for over 2 years and other cruel treatment including being kept naked, blindfolded, shackled and wearing ear plugs for months. Every one of these tactics is against the law in America. Because of his pain and suffering, he confessed to a minor crime, in which he was convicted, instead of the more serious crimes of terrorist activities.

It isn't very often that the opportunity comes along where a teacher can take a real life controversial topic and turn it into a fiery, challenging and academic lesson. In this case, the students were in shock that this document they thought seemed reasonable and fair may not be fair at all.

When the students took on this assignment, they were asked to support their answer with information from the handout. Most wrote one page. Every student was in agreement that the U. S. Constitution does not necessarily offer what it says it does to every citizen.

I hung this assignment outside my room in the 5th and 6th grade pod area with an explanation of the assignment along with the handout. A few weeks later, I took my class to a one week outdoor school, called Camp Waskowitz. While we were gone, the principal brought his boss into the pod to visit some classrooms. When they came to my student's work posted on the wall the principal's boss stopped and read every single paper. They both were amazed at the assignment and the thoughtful effort of the kids.

Chapter 14

Some Favorite Lessons and Projects

During my first year teaching 6th grade, I realized my style of bringing fun and silliness into the classroom motivated the students to have a more positive attitude toward learning. There was a correlation between my antics and craziness and the students' efforts and grades. I felt like a scientist in a laboratory who was experimenting with ingredients of laughter and fun. As I served up those ingredients, they were immediately transformed into scholars who wanted to be challenged more! I couldn't have been more surprised! So I added "challenge" into my other ingredients. I found the perfect blend for student success was to have fun and laughter along with lessons and projects that engaged and challenged the kids.

You can teach a math lesson about graphing from the textbook, using a word problem and graph paper. Or you can teach the same required math standard in a way that engages the students and at the same time will help them retain what you are teaching.

When it came time for the students to learn about graphing, they split up into groups of three. They then agreed upon a research question, such as *what is your favorite school subject?* Or *what is your favorite cafeteria meal?* They typed their question followed by all the possible answers including one for "other".

Next they made copies of their questions and choices for answers and went around to the 4th, 5th and 6th grade classrooms (including ours) and distributed the half-page sheets, along with instructions to the students. I had already emailed the teachers to determine the best time to come by and have their class complete this short survey.

As each group returned to my class, they tallied their results and then constructed 4 different types of graphs with the data they collected: a line plot, a bar graph, a line graph and a pie chart.

Each group then explained to our class their research question and showed the graph results on the overhead projector. Although this graphing lesson required more time, it added teamwork, additional critical thinking skills, research and group presentation for this lesson.

One of my favorite lessons was teaching the students how to become better writers when using dialog. I wanted them to discover there are more descriptive words to use besides "said". So as a class, we brainstormed other words for "said".

As the kids raised their hands, one student was chosen to write these alternative words on the white board. They could not look in their reading books or go on a computer. When we got to 90 words, I challenged the class to reach 100. They did!

I have never before taught a lesson which resulted in almost 100% individual volunteer participation, but this one almost always achieved that amazing goal. When the kids looked at 6 or 7 columns of words for "said" on the board, they were amazed at their accomplishment. The words were then copied onto several posters and hung on the wall for the students to refer to during writing assignments. They also received a handout titled, *Other words for "said"* which could be used for writing homework.

After the brainstorm session, I taught a brief lesson on how to punctuate dialog. The students then had to complete a writing assignment in which they could choose from four different story titles needing conversation. My favorite topic was asking someone out on a date. They were not allowed to use "said", but rather a more appropriate word which described the tone of the conversation. For example, if a person was raising his or her voice, they could use *screamed, yelled, shouted, etc.* Not only was this an effective writing lesson, but it boosted their self-esteem because of the total group's contribution.

When I retired from teaching and became a sub, I would occasionally teach this lesson with the teacher's permission. One year I introduced it to a 6th grade challenge class. In about 40 minutes, they generated 205 words to replace "said". When their teacher returned the following day, she was completely mesmerized when she noticed the words, which we left on the board, and the feelings of accomplishment which glowed on the faces of the students.

One required lesson in writing is about comparing and contrasting: determining what is the same and what is different in two stories. I discovered a short story called *The Yellow Handkerchief*, which was about a convict who was released from jail and taking a bus back to his hometown where he hoped his girlfriend would take him back. He told her in a letter he would know her answer was yes if she tied a yellow handkerchief around the oak tree in her yard. If no handkerchief was there, he would know the answer was no and he would keep going.

After reading this story, it reminded me of the 1973 smash hit by Tony Orlando and Dawn called, *Tie a Yellow Ribbon 'Round the Old Oak Tree*. I realized there were both similarities and differences in the story and song. I made copies from the lyrics of the worldwide hit song and the short story. What the students did not yet know, however, was that the song writer was sued by the author of the short story for stealing his ideas.

Part one of this lesson was reading the story together and then listening to the song. Because the song had such a catchy melody, many of the students responded by dancing in their seats and asking me to replay the hit song several times. After the class discussed both the story and the lyrics to the song, they each had to record the similarities and differences between the two. When they completed this assignment, I wrote their answers on the board. I wanted the class to see an inclusive list so they would be able to factually analyze the lawsuit as if they were a member of the jury.

Almost every student felt there were too many similarities for the lyrics to be coincidental and voted in favor of the plaintiff, the author. They could not believe or comprehend the verdict. The judge ruled in favor of the defendant by saying that it was not uncommon for someone to tie something yellow around a tree to express a positive feeling and therefore it was not plagiarism. This assignment was one of my favorites and I taught it several times when principals were in my room for my annual evaluation. It's another good example of taking a required lesson and molding it into a fun and challenging assignment, which culminated with a jury discussion from an actual case.

In 6th grade math, students learn how to calculate sales tax and tipping. Rather than using the uninspiring lesson from the book, I went to an Italian restaurant and asked if they would donate 30 "takeout" menus for a math lesson I was teaching to my 6th graders. They happily agreed and I had my new textbook.

I told my classes we were all going to eat dinner at an Italian restaurant (in the pretend world). They would be sitting in booths with 3-4 of their friends and classmates. I passed out the menus and told them to order as if they were hungry, but to keep it "real". They wrote down their complete order, which included soup, salad, entrée, drink and dessert and the price of each item. After totaling their bill, I then explained how sales tax worked and asked them to add in the sales tax amount. We then discussed the concept and calculation of tipping and that amount was also added to their bill.

Then I told them their parents just called and requested they bring home a medium pepperoni pizza and to calculate their new bill total. Next they each calculated the total for their entire table for both tax and tip and then for the whole class. The prop made the lesson more real and fun. The only negative was that I had to listen to them complain about hunger pains and why couldn't I take the whole class out for pizza.

Chapter 15

Some Great Principals

I've been very fortunate in that I have had some really amazing principals. I have been able to have fun with them while at the same time gain their respect for my teaching effectiveness and my style. One Christmas, our principal Mr.Dave gave each staff member a card with a wallet size picture of himself and a note on the back saying if we ever need inspiration, "hopefully this picture will provide that extra spark".

I immediately knew there would be retaliation on my part when we returned from Christmas break. At our next staff meeting I gave a box, addressed to Dave, to the librarian to give to him before our meeting started. She read my card which said, "Dave, I really appreciated your Christmas card and especially the picture of yourself. Since returning from the Holiday Break, I've used it as you recommended, when I was having a difficult day. I wanted to reciprocate your consideration and hope this gift will be able to provide an uplift for you when your day isn't going well. Just remember, you always need to think big."

Our librarian then had Dave open his gift box. Inside was a poster size picture of me. The reaction from the staff was so amazing, I actually got a standing ovation. He even hung my poster in his office for the balance of the school year.

After 9 years as my principal, Dave transferred to another school and Mark was hired as his replacement. I thought it would be a good idea for me to talk to Mark and explain some of my unconventional teaching methods. At the same time, I would make him aware of their effectiveness and of the amazing relationships I had with the parents of my students.

I told him I did not use the required textbook of short stories for reading, but had formulated a collection of other stories which I was convinced offered greater teaching material. These would engage the students at a higher level, incorporate life in the real world and result in higher scores on the state test at the end of the year. I also told him how I challenged the students in math and also discussed the importance of giving math homework based on what was taught in class that day rather than a weekly math packet.

He responded by saying he would continue to let me teach my way, but I would be under his microscope during the course of the current year. He also told me that if my scores were not satisfactory at the end of the year, I would have to teach in the more conventional manner. I had confidence in my style, my ability and my lessons, but was still concerned about the challenges that faced me. I thought it might be an incentive to my class if they knew what was at stake. They assured me they would give an extra effort so my curriculum and my teaching style could continue after they graduated.

When the new teaching year started in September, Mark called me into his office and closed his door. You always get nervous when your boss closes the door. I sat down, not knowing what to think, when Mark said, "Congratulations Jim". It's good to get a compliment, but I did not have a clue what the compliment was for. I thanked him and then asked what I had done. He proceeded to tell me that when the state test scores were reported back to the school in math and reading, he used his own formula for determining the effectiveness of each teacher. Part of his formula was to compare the scores from the prior year and see if the student made gains with their new teacher.

Everyone likes to receive praise whether from the teacher to the student, from the teacher to another teacher or especially from the principal to the teacher. What Mark said to me next, were words that made my day. "Jim, you had the highest scores in reading and math than any other teacher in our school". I then asked him if this meant I could continue to teach my way, employing my unorthodox methods. He replied, "Jim, you can do whatever you want". Those are words that no teacher ever expects to hear.

One year I had my students create a brochure on the computer for a health project. We were learning about addictions to drugs, tobacco and alcohol. I thought this subject matter was critically important as their lives got more complicated and temptations became harder to ignore. I gave a lesson on why brochures are a useful tool for communicating information and the methods to having an effective brochure.

The final drafts of the student's brochures were so spectacular I displayed them in a glass showcase outside the office. I was hoping to get positive feedback from the principal so I could pass it on to the kids, but he did not respond. A few days later, I asked him if he had a chance to look them over. His reaction was the highest possible compliment one could ever hope to hear. He told me that he did see them and the information, design and impact was so good he just assumed they were done professionally and put up by the counselor.

Two years later Mark was sent to a middle school. His assistant principal, Felicia, returned as our new principal. She was another principal who was very good at her job and believed it was important to laugh and have fun during the course of your work day. When teacher evaluations are completed by Felicia, she meets with the teacher to review their performance. Since I did not hear from her for several weeks, I sent her the following e-mail:

Hello Felicia,

We have not gotten together to discuss my observation yet. Please check the appropriate box below to reply:

- ❏ *You're so easy to forget, I forgot about you.*
- ❏ *Since it was your last year teaching, no one really cares.*
- ❏ *It was so bad, it wouldn't do any good to discuss the lesson, because there is no hope.*
- ❏ *It was so good, it wouldn't do any good to discuss the lesson, because you are perfect.*
- ❏ *I was waiting to surprise you that you have been selected by NBC to host a new math reality show.*
- ❏ *I was trying to figure out how to tell you that Tammy Vo, who achieved a perfect score on the State MSP test, is replacing you.*
- ❏ *Other _____*

Please respond at your earlier convenience.

Sincerely,
Jim

Following is Felicia's answer:

*Those are all **Hilarious – folks don't know why I'm laughing so hard.***

- *It was so good, it wouldn't do any good to discuss the lesson because you are perfect.*

You are my priority tomorrow morning, I have not forgotten about you ---Felicia

Thank you Dave, thank you Mark and thank you Felicia for your leadership, guidance and believing that fun and humor can also be part of the teaching process.

Chapter 16

Field Trips

Field trips are an integral part of student learning. After a couple of years teaching 6th grade, I thought about taking the 6th grade classes to Safeco Field to see the Seattle Mariners play an afternoon game. I thought this would be unique, but also educational. My only roadblock would be selling this idea to my principal. I formulated a convincing plan that consisted of 5 components.

The first was to get the students pumped and primed for what would follow in the classroom the day after the game. Upon returning to school the next day, everything that was taught during the next week would have a baseball theme. We read about Jackie Robinson. For social studies, we studied segregation in baseball. We read the famous poem by Grantland Rice, *Casey At The Bat* and then I had the kids write their own baseball poems. Part of math became baseball word problems. Science became the study of how to make a baseball curve.

The second component to convince Dave this was a viable idea was to make him aware that everything we taught satisfied required frameworks. I listed the frameworks and their numbers.

The third component was that this strategy would motivate the kids to complete their baseball assignments with more enthusiasm and a greater effort. It is easy to get caught up in the excitement of a baseball game and for many, this would be a first time experience. The next step was to transfer that excitement to their school work

The fourth component was to have the opportunity to teach some unique lessons, such as the concept of eminent domain (when the city can purchase land from a landlord even if they don't want to sell, because it will benefit the community). We had some great discussions in which I proposed a scenario where a couple owned a dry cleaning store or a small market and did not want to lose their business. However, the city needed to acquire property, including theirs, in order to build a stadium. They were forced to sell, like it or not, because the stadium would benefit the community. The city, of course, would have to pay them a fair price. Few teachers would think to have a discussion where young kids are encouraged to debate a very real, but controversial subject.

The last component of my plan was to say thank you to these 6th graders for being exceptional students and leaders by their mature and thoughtful behavior. It was a great way to reward their efforts in a special way.

We had a fundraiser, for students who could not afford the price of the ticket (which was reduced by the Seattle Mariners) and to raise some extra cash for food and drinks.

After I presented my proposal to Dave, he was on board. However, something like this needed the approval of the school district. Dave used my convincing arguments and we got our approval.

After a few years, the district changed its stand on our afternoon game. They said it did not fulfill the educational purpose of a field trip and we could no longer go during school hours. They did, however, say we could go as a group during a night game which we did for the duration of my teaching career. I thought it was odd that the district would sanction our game at night when it is dark and there was potential for more things to go wrong. When you're in a place with 40,000 people (many drinking beer) and the kids are going out to get snacks and go to the restroom, you would think the school district would prefer to sanction this event during daylight hours.

Whenever we could, we tried to schedule field trips that were appropriate to 6th grade students. After several years of teaching, the school counselor suggested we take all 6th graders to check out the University of Washington. She contacted a department that arranged for selected grades to see various facilities of the college such as a lecture hall, a lab, dormitory, library, and the student union. Even though the students are 6 years away from attending a university, it proved to be a successful and informative field trip to start the juices flowing. Part of our tour included the various types of scholarships and how to apply for student loans.

While many 6th graders were impressed with seeing college life up close, we knew this form of higher education was not for everyone. We therefore added a second field trip (third counting our baseball game) to a vocational school called Puget Sound Skill Center (PSSC). This program was offered to high school students who were at least sophomores. It consisted of attending core subjects at the home high school either in the morning or afternoon. The students were then bused to PSSC for the other half of the day to choose a career path in several different courses including: web design, construction, translation, fashion design, medical assisting, dental assisting, law enforcement, firefighting, culinary arts, computer courses and several other programs to choose from.

In small groups, the students were able to tour several of the classrooms and ask the students and teacher questions pertaining to the specific course. We even got to eat lunch in the dining hall where the food was prepared by the culinary arts students.

These two field trips educated our 6th graders on two different avenues of attaining a higher education degree.

There are very few elementary schools who chose these two field trips, but they were wildly successful in planting the seeds for two very different career options.

On a couple of occasions, I took my 6th grade class to see the process of how the Seattle Times newspaper was printed. During the next few weeks, I read a book to the students about a girl who as a 6th grader, decided to publish a newspaper with the help of some of her fellow students. After I finished the book, the class then embarked on publishing the Mount View Gazette which was distributed to their parents, all 4th, 5th and 6th grade students and all school staff.

Since I am low-tech, I was unable to formulate the newspaper on a computer, so the various articles had to be cut and pasted the old fashioned way – with scissors and glue. It was formatted on several pages using 11 by 17 paper. Included were world and U. S. news, Seattle news, Mount View news, sports, movie reviews, book reviews, editorials and classifieds. I remember that one of my students tried to sell his younger brother in the classified section. The students worked in small groups of 3-4 after choosing which section they would write about. The field trip and reading the book to the class helped to propel the students into publishing their own successful newspaper with great raves from parents, students and staff.

Field trips can become an important extension of the classroom by putting students in new surroundings, such as the zoo, a salmon hatchery, a museum, a science center and so many other interesting learning environments. While many field trips are free, teachers are prevented from taking their classes on too many of these excursions due to the cost of buses. Since these usually run about $250 for the school bus, most teachers are limited to just one or two field trips each school year.

Chapter 17

T-shirts, Spirit Days and Uniforms

One accomplishment that I'm really proud of was my idea to have the entire student body submit designs for t-shirts, which were then sold to kids, parents and staff. I got my idea when the school decided to purchase shirts with their tiger mascot and school name. Although this was a good spirit builder for the students and staff, I felt there was an opportunity here to get the students involved in the design process and sell them for a profit to the school.

It took several months for this idea to develop in my head, but when school started the following year, I was ready to roll it out. I created a t-shirt template on an 8 ½ x 11 sheet of paper where students could design, in pencil, a picture of a tiger with Mount View written on the template. I divided the school into 3 competing groups: K, 1st, 2nd grades; 3rd and 4th grades and 5th and 6th grades. All designs had to be original and fill the majority of the template.

Like anything that involves art, the majority of people are not very artistic, but for this project, some of the best designs were done by 1st and 2nd graders where the cuteness factor was sometimes more endearing than the true art of the 4th, 5th and 6th graders. My plan was to have 23 teachers help choose the best 3 designs for each group. These 9 designs became the semifinalists. The templates were reduced in size and placed on a voting sheet which was circulated to the student body and staff. The instructions were: If you were to purchase a shirt from each group, which shirt would you buy.

After the voting sheets were returned to me, the t-shirt committee tallied the results. If the vote was really close between 2 shirts in a group, we chose both. Next, we created a purchase order with pictures of the winning designs that would be printed on white t-shirts with a listing of adult and child sizes. The winners received a free shirt and the self-esteem that went along with seeing dozens of kids and adults wearing their design.

Each year we usually sold 125 to 150 shirts which raised about $400 in profit for the school. The students wore these throughout the week, but we set every other Friday as an official T-shirt day.

Many schools have spirit days. Pajama day, mismatch day, sports day are all common and well received by the staff and kids. But Mount View wanted to expand the concept and formulated about 12-13 spirit days on every other Friday.

I can't remember them all, but in addition to those I mentioned above, we also had tie dye day, polka dot and stripe day, character in a book day, island day, hat day, bling day, twin day and cowboy day.

I personally put my heart and soul into spirit days. On mismatched day, I actually shaved off half of my mustache and half of my beard on opposite sides. I had gone to Supercuts the previous day and had them cut my facial hair. I learned to ignore the stares, but if anybody asked me "why", I had a great story to tell. After spirit day ended, I drove back to Supercuts and had my half mustache and beard shaved off.

Another personal favorite was tie dye day. I had a great T-shirt as did many kids and teachers. But in order to take it to a higher level, I tie-dyed my light blue jeans to match the shirt and then added the final touch by coloring my beard to match the shirt and jeans.

For "character in a book" day, I chose to go as Viola Swamp from the book *Miss Nelson Is Missing*. I went to Goodwill and bought a black dress that closely resembled the book character, a pair of women's shoes I could walk in and a wig that copied Viola's hair style. Fred Meyer provided the exact same color-striped high socks and the final touch came from one of my wife's bras stuffed with a pair of my gym socks. I would like to give a special thanks to Marjean, a para educator who helped me perfect a woman's walk. The best part was when the bra/socks started slipping downward, I would grab my chest and push them back up. This was done in class, the hallway and anywhere else, evoking giggles and laughter from students and teachers.

Shortly before I retired, at a year-end assembly, a few staff members presented a slide show of all my dress up days. As the students were laughing and clapping, I was wiping away a few tears, thinking about all the great memories and all the good times I was leaving behind.

As the yearbook coordinator, I took hundreds of pictures, which created terrific memories for the kids to have and look back on. In addition to educating the kids, schools also need to provide interesting events, unique social situations and fun and zany memories. I'm sad to say that when I retired, the T-shirt program and spirit days were discontinued for a time and the yearbook was only published a few times after my retirement.

Not only were these spirit builders gone, but the school went in the opposite direction and required all students to wear school uniforms. It was discussed the prior year with the final decision coming from the votes of parents. I was one of only two staff members who opposed uniforms. I strongly believed the parents were under the impression that uniforms would increase student scores, but there was no evidence to support that claim. It did, however, take away the students' individuality, which I felt was an important component in expressing oneself.

When I came back to Mount View in subsequent years to sub and I looked out at the students in class and saw nothing but "sameness", it was very discouraging and sad to me. If I were still teaching, I think I actually would have transferred to a different school in the district if I had a few years left to teach.

Chapter 18

Some Interesting Pictures, Posters And A Pencil Graveyard

Each classroom had a library of about 600 books that were categorized by genre and reading level. I felt I needed something on the wall to encourage the students to read. It didn't take long to find an answer. I had a cushioned chair with a matching ottoman at home. I also had a trainable dog, a book, a book holder and a camera. I got the dog to sit on the chair. I chose a book titled, *The Universe for The Beginner* and placed it in the holder and the holder on the ottoman. I then took about 25 pictures of my dog, Smudge, until I got one that looked exactly like he was deeply engrossed in the book!

I had the picture blown up to poster size and framed in a thin wooden frame. The caption read, *If my dog Smudge can read for 20 minutes each day, then you certainly can do the same.* I don't know if this hanging poster got more kids to read, but at least I could brag that I had the smartest dog of any student or teacher in the school.

Years later I took a picture of my daughter's dog looking through a telescope. I had this picture along with the one of Smudge reading a book, sealed together side by side on foam board with the printed caption, *Which dog is smarter? The one who looks at the stars or the one who reads about them?*

One thing I noticed in the teacher's rooms was a list of rules posted on the wall. It was necessary, but I wanted my posted rules to be less lengthy, but complete and more impactful. So I created a poster that was in the front of the class for everyone to see each day. It was titled ONE SIMPLE RULE and in strategic writing said:

One Simple Rule:

You All Know the Difference Between What Is Right and What Is Wrong

So Please Follow My One Rule

"Think Before You Act"

It certainly satisfied my requirements for a behavior poster: brief, complete and impactful. I honestly believe it had a greater positive effect than the other longer list of teacher's rules. I had a student named Peter who contacted me about 10 years after he graduated and told me that one of the most powerful things I did was to create this one rule, which really said it all. He told me he frequently read this before he engaged in any questionable behavior.

When a teacher gets this type of feedback, not only does it make them feel good, but it also reinforces the magnitude of whatever it was they did. If my simple rule had that kind of effect on Peter, there's a good chance it did the same for many other students.

So now you might be wondering about the last part of the title of this chapter, Pencil Graveyard. About my 5th year of teaching, I walked into a 4th grade teachers room and noticed she had some very short pencils scotch taped on her wall with a sheet of paper that referred to them as Pencil Cemetery. It was only there for one year, but I knew it had great potential and all I had to do was expand on her idea.

I had noticed many students had created some very short pencils. They used the hand held plastic sharpeners to get sharp writing points. With Vivienne's idea and my desire to expand on it, I created my Pencil Graveyard. I drew a template of a curved headstone about 3 inches tall and glued 36 of them onto a large black poster board with the title: **Pencil Graveyard.** My wife and I then wrote a few examples of a short 4-line poem like:

> Here lies Dixon
> Number two.
> I'm sorry that
> Your Life is through.

Using double sided tape, we typed and cut our examples and then taped them onto the headstones. I then taped a very short pencil under each headstone. We put the white blank headstones on the rest of the poster and hung it on the wall. I told the students they could add their pencil or a classmate's, but their pencil would have to be accompanied by a short 4-line poem. I also stated I would have to proofread their poem before they typed and cut it out. We talked about the flow of a poem and the correct syntax.

Within a few weeks, the entire poster was covered in short pencils with a personal poem about how each pencil's life had come to an end. There was one requirement that the pencil could not exceed one inch in length and it had to be able to write. Pretty soon, word got out about my poster to other classrooms and during the day I would occasionally have a first or second grader come upstairs to my room, hand me a short pencil and tell me it was for my pencil graveyard.

Following are some examples of epitaphs for pencils who have been laid to rest. (Remember they are written by 11 and 12 year old kids).

> You used to draw
> You would erase
> But now it's time
> To be replaced.
> > Victoria

> Here lies a pencil
> All old and short.
> You're no longer able
> To write a book report.
> > Michele

> When I got you
> I said hi.
> When you went to the grave
> I said bye.
> > Thai

Jim Seaman

Once you were clean,
Smooth and gold.
Now you have bite marks
Scratches and mold.
           Adriel

Before you had
A lot of lead
But now you are
Skinny and dead
               Kennith

You used to be tall
And very bold
But now you are tiny
And to short to hold
               Chris

Here's one that I wrote and read to the class, just for kicks:

> Where oh where has all my lead gone?
> Maybe to Tucson or up to the Yukon
> Maybe Taiwan or the Amazon
> Maybe Saigon or to Babylon
>
>
> Who oh who made my lead be gone?
> Was it Yvonne, or Ron or Don?
> What about Juan or John or maybe the ex-con
> Maybe the leprechaun or slithering python
> But not to worry, I've got a market coupon!

After the first year, I took the poems off the headstones and removed the pencils. This gave me extra pencils in case some students could not or did not want to go through the sharpening process. I used this poster for the remaining years that I taught and never got tired of seeing the kids' pencils or their poems. When I retired I took the best poems and the best of the pencils (both of which I had kept), and created one last pencil graveyard which hangs in my office at home.

Chapter 19

Some More Lessons and Projects

One year, I finished teaching the required curriculum with about 2 weeks before the students had to take the state tests. Most teachers do some serious review, especially in math, to hopefully increase the student's test scores. Not only are the scores a reflection of how each student did for the year in reading and math, but these scores are also a reflection of the teacher's abilities and effectiveness.

So I broke up math into a morning session, which focused on reviewing the year's math frameworks and an afternoon session which consisted of teams of two students creating a math board game. The concepts were simple: a board, dice or spinner or other method to advance the tokens, cards with questions on one side and the answers on the back and directions for the game. They used the math book to identify the frameworks, but had to make up their own problems, including some word problems.

As teams finished their board game, they played another team's game. This enabled them to achieve a minimum of 3 different reviews: the basic math book morning review, the research of problems and answers for their own game and playing at least one other team's game. I only did this once, because there usually isn't enough time at the end of the year. It is almost impossible to teach the entire required curriculum, but this one year, it seemed that everything came together.

I was very curious to see the student's test scores to determine if there was any correlation between the extra fun review and what I normally do. The answer is the test scores were some of the highest I have attained as a teacher. If other teachers are reading this, please take notice that fun and creative projects can put the students in a good place mentally which in turn translates to better understanding of the material taught and better performance on tests.

Each year, I implemented my Bill Gates number review. I told the class I had to run to the bathroom and I would be right back. About a minute later, I walked back in wearing a Bill Gates mask. I told the class Mr. Seaman would be delayed and he asked me to take over his class. Most of the kids recognized me as a Bill Gates stand-in, as I introduced myself to the class as the famous billionaire. I posed the question to the class: which would you rather have, one million dollars or a penny the first day, with each day's amount doubled thereafter for a period of one month. I even made up a fake million dollar bill which I called a "Mill Bill" and handed it out to those who chose the one million dollars. The majority of students always took the million dollars.

The students were then asked to complete the math to see if they made the correct choice. When they were done with their calculations, the total amount for choosing the ever-growing pennies for 30 days was a whopping $7,395,082.24.

This was simply a multiplication review, but the questioning, thinking and decision making it created for the students, made for an exciting and fun-filled lesson.

I was always very project minded, more so than most teachers. Projects enable the student to combine several learning skills into completing a fun assignment. Fifth grade social studies in the state of Washington is based around the U. S. and required the students to learn about colonial times and the industrial revolution up to the civil war. History, with its dates, times and places can be a bit boring for students. I only taught 5th grade twice, so I wasn't really prepared with many projects that would inspire, engage and teach the kids. But in my quest to do so, I did conceive one of my favorite projects.

I named the project *Road Trippin' 'Round the USA*. It consisted of learning how to read classified ads, use and understand symbols on a map and calculate auto mileage. The students also explored internet research, geography, decision making, journal and narrative writing, creating tables and paraphrasing. This project centered around the premise that the students won $100,000 in the Washington State Lottery and in teams of two, decided to buy a car and travel around the United States to see historical landmarks.

I went to Pemco Insurance Company and, after I explained my project, they were eager to give me 15 maps of the U.S. Whenever possible, I like to have the parents be both aware and involved in what is going on in class. Homework for the first night of this assignment was for the students to review the project handout with mom and dad and have them sign off on it.

The students were given a list of 23 historical sights and their location by state. With their U. S. map, they had to plan the best itinerary from Seattle. Some of the sites were Mount Rushmore, Denver Mint, Grand Canyon, Kitty Hawk, Alamo, Texas Book Depository, Vietnam Veterans Memorial, Ford's Theater and the United Nations.

They were required to keep a journal and a chart of expenses for gas, meals and souvenirs. After they visited a historical site, they researched the site, writing a half page or more in their journal about its history using the journalistic questions: *what, where, when, why, who, how.* They also printed a picture of the historical site and glued it into their journal.

The students were particularly interested in seeing photos and reading about where President Kennedy was assassinated. They were also excited to see where money is made and visit the United Nations. They took pride in planning the quickest routes for their journey and had fun deciding what automobile to purchase. The school year was quickly coming to a close so there was not enough time to travel to each and every landmark and research them, but what was accomplished by each team was beyond amazing. This was the end of the school year when students started running out of gas and started to shut down. But *Road Trippin' 'Round the USA*, provided the students with the interest and motivation to keep learning and working at their highest level.

If you want students to learn narrative writing, you teach them all the components of the lesson. If you want students to understand geography, you give them maps and teach them how to read the key. If you want to teach students how to research a topic, you take them into the computer lab and give them a tutorial. But when you want to reinforce a teaching standard, why not create a project which encompasses many different standards? There is no better way to engage students and make learning fun than project based learning.

One subject that is required throughout elementary school is teaching facts and opinions. It is always interesting to read how students reach an opinion on a controversial subject. In 5th and 6th grade, a common lesson is to have the students read articles about the pros and cons of having chocolate milk in school. It is certainly something that the kids can relate to and then write an essay on their opinion providing details to support their conclusion.

But I've always felt it's best to use a subject with more substance and impact, thereby allowing the students to be challenged in topics that are more meaningful and historical. So when it came to 6th grade opinions, I used some very controversial subjects for editorial writing.

I decided to implement a topic that I have struggled with for many years: *the death penalty.* When I researched the internet for articles that presented each side, I was unable to find ones that were kid friendly and also had the details I was looking for. So, with information about pros and cons, I wrote two articles with two differing sides.

We read them in class and had some amazing discussions and debates. Just about everyone in class had something to say. The students listened attentively to what others had to say. Some arguments were so convincing, many students changed their minds. After two days of discussions, each student wrote their opinion providing details to support their reasoning on this very adult topic.

Another adult topic I chose for this curriculum was: *Should the U.S. have dropped the atomic bomb on Japan to end World War II, killing over 250,000 civilians.* For this assignment, I had the kids work in groups of 4 and do their own research about the pros and cons. They took notes to provide their group with adequate information. They discussed both sides and then wrote their own editorial.

In both of these assignments, I asked for a few volunteers to read their essays to the class. The students listened attentively and then politely asked valid questions. When I taught in this manner, I observed pre-teens elevate their critical thinking skills to those of young mature adults.

Chapter 20

How to Make Reading More Fun

In the school district in which I taught, the required reading textbook was called Open Court. It was a collection of short stories and included a teacher's book with lessons and activities. There were different books for each grade level. Each unit had 6-7 stories about a specific theme. For example, there was a theme about perseverance which included several stories about people who did not give up until they achieved their dreams and goals.

From the student's standpoint, all the stories had one thing in common. They were boring. In my district, it was required that 90 minutes be spent each day on reading which included independent reading, reading aloud, vocabulary, word study and other lessons. I soon realized if you wanted students to have passion for reading, it would certainly help if the stories were interesting, exciting and maybe even fun.

If you want to have lessons about cause and effect, dialog, opinions or the numerous other required frameworks, there are many other short stories that would do a better job of engaging the students. So with the principal's blessing, I set out to discover books over the summer that satisfied the curriculum and also my own criteria – interesting, exciting, and fun.

I began to rack up short stories of high interest! *It's All About Pee*, which told how pee was used in soaps, how you are supposed to pee on a jellyfish sting to stop the pain, how soldiers dressed in armor in medieval times were able to pee and other fascinating informative pee stories; or *Mistaken Identity*, a story about two girls who looked remarkably the same. As they were both returning from a job, they were in an accident. One was killed and the other badly injured with severe facial injuries. When the identification cards of the two girls got mixed up, both sets of parents were given the wrong information. The parents of the girl who survived were told their daughter had died and the parents of the girl that died were told she survived. A fascinating story, which was documented on 20/20.

Through My Eyes, was the story of Ruby Bridges who was one of 2 black girls who were integrated into an all-white elementary school in 1960. *The Most Dangerous Game*, was a fiction story about boats that crashed into jagged rocks off an island, forcing the survivors to swim to land. The island was inhabited solely by a hunter who was bored with hunting animals and wanted the challenge of hunting humans. *I Escaped a Violent Gang*, was about an eleven year old girl who joined a hard core gang and at age 15 fought to get out. I hoped this true story would have a lasting impact for my students about the horrors of gang life and the very real possibility of prison or death. The story was made into a 2007 movie titled *Freedom Writers* which starred Hilary Swank. (An amazing film that everyone needs to see if they haven't) Another story was about a Japanese family interned in a prison camp during WWII titled, *I am an American.* All of these stories and the many others I had students read, had one thing in common. They engaged the students and were interesting or exciting.

Most of the stories were not only true, but also impactful and/or educational for the students both in reading skills and the American history. Eventually, the district got away from the required reading material and allowed for teacher choice books as long as the required lessons were taught. It was good to be several years ahead of the district's lack of connecting the dots.

Many teachers would have the students write a book report after they completed reading a book of their choice. Most of you have probably done that in various grades. It usually consisted of a detailed summary and maybe a recommendation or rating of the book. I came up with a more extensive report. For lack of a better name, I called it a *Different Kind Of Book Report.* The students were given a list of 18 different assignments. They were required to complete 2 from the list. The first was to add another adventure or conflict. The second was to choose a main character in the story and predict what their life would be like in the future. In addition, they had to choose any 5 other assignments from the list of 18.

Some of these choices were: Introduce a new character: compare a character to yourself: come up with three other titles and explain why you chose them; create a comic strip for a story segment; write a book review; write a summary for a sequel or write a summary for a prequel. The above options were much more engaging and challenging than writing the typical book report.

Seattle isn't known for its sunny weather, but occasionally during the school year, there would be some nice days with balmy weather. On these spring days, I would take the kids outside to sit on the bleachers or lay on the grass and read or write. They knew if they played around or got off task, they could spoil it for the whole class. And of course the whole class would know who was responsible for everyone losing their outside privileges.

I always felt, as important as reading is, the district might have placed a little too much emphasis on this one subject. In class, teachers would do read alouds to students for 15-20 minutes; the students would then have to read silently a book of their choice for 20-30 minutes each day; there would be a reading lesson on a specific story; there would be a lesson on word study and additionally the students would be reading in every other subject throughout the day including word problems in math. At home, it was required that students read for 20-30 minutes and have their parents sign their reading log.

When students graduate from high school, the majority are able to read at a level in which they can function well enough to live a productive life in society. But too many are deficient in writing, too many don't know what is going on in the world and too many don't have the skills to excel at a high level in society. I'm sure I'm one of the very few teachers to feel this way about reading, but think about what I'm saying and ask yourself if other areas of learning are being short changed.

I found it very productive to break up this required 2 hour reading block of time. Common sense tells me that it is very difficult for adults, much less students in grades 1-6, to stay attentive for 2 hours in a reading assignment, then go directly into another reading lesson and another and another. Not to mention reading throughout the day in other subjects.

Chapter 21

The Kids

For a teacher, it's always about the kids. Throughout the years, I've had angels, high achievers, special education students, newcomers to our country, students with extremely low self esteem, students who had been sexually abused and numerous other challenges.

It's important that teachers know the strengths and weaknesses of every student. For those kids who put up walls, the teacher needs to find a way to break through them. For those who excel, the teacher needs to challenge them and take them to a higher level. For those who are average, the teacher needs to encourage striving for improvement.

This happens best if the teacher has a special connection with each student and can develop a partnership with the parents. One year I had a student who got 100% on 7 consecutive reading comprehension tests. I challenged him to study a little harder so he could keep his streak going. When he told his parents about his scores, they were so impressed, his dad said he would give him $50.00 if he got 100% on his next reading test. After the next test, Francisco was $50.00

richer. All good things usually come to an end and so did Francisco's streak. But for several weeks, the students, his parents and myself were all cheering him on.

In that same class, another student realized a special accomplishment. Trey always gave such a valiant effort in every assignment and test, but he couldn't make that breakthrough to get him into the 90% range. Then one day as I was handing back a math test to the class, I heard Trey shout out, "I just got my first 100% in my life!" I knew he had received a perfect score, but I had no idea it was a milestone for him. What happened next was an amazing reaction from the entire class. When they heard his exclamation about his first ever 100%, they all cheered and clapped and responded in a way that added to Trey's happy moment.

A few years later I had a student by the name of Lisa who consistently received high scores.

But rather than having her accomplishments come naturally or easily, she worked hard for them.

She soon tied Francisco's record of 8 consecutive scores of 100% on reading comprehension tests. I told her about this record and challenged her to break it. After she achieved her 9th perfect score, she went on to accomplish something that I'm sure is very very rare. At the end of the school year, she attained 100% 's on 22 consecutive reading tests. These comprehension tests are not easy. They are mostly questions where you have to give details to support your answer. At the end of the school year, I asked Lisa how she was able to accomplish this feat. She answered that she had set a goal, after several 100's, to not miss one question on her reading tests for the rest of the year.

I told my students that whenever they take a test that asks for 3 details, they should always give 4. If it asks for 4, try to give 5. This way if one of your details is incorrect, you can still receive the maximum points on that question. Whenever I handed back reading tests, I always chose a few examples of students who did this and put their test on the overhead. This way, the class could see that they went from a B to an A or a C to a B because they followed my suggestion.

I wanted Lisa to feel that her accomplishment was spectacular and even though I gave her high fives, low fives, fist bumps and whatever else was "in" at the time, I wanted something bigger for her. I told the principal about her 22 perfect test scores for the entire year and asked him if he would come to the class and congratulate her. He agreed and after he commended her achievement the entire class clapped and cheered.

One year, when I taught 5th grade, I had a student from South Korea. When I found out he only knew a handful of English words, I had no idea what I was going to do. In 12 years of teaching, I had never been put in this challenging position. In prior years, the ESL (English as a Second Language) students were in self-contained classrooms with 2-3 different grades. But this arrangement was later changed and these students were mainstreamed into classes with their own grade. Para educators worked with them both in small groups outside the class and also in their regular classrooms.

I went to the ESL coordinator and asked her for suggestions on how I could teach Bumsock when he was not working in small groups with the para. Since many ESL students having limited knowledge of our language are from Mexico or Vietnam, they can receive help from their classmates who are from those countries. But I have never had another student from South Korea, so that strategy was not an option.

I did use two very effective tools, however. The first was a South Korean to English dictionary, which showed colored pictures of nouns. The second was a computer program in which I could type a sentence in English, hit a button and see it translated into South Korean. I gave Bumsock a list of 7-8 nouns each day and had him look up the English spelling with the picture. He then wrote the word several times in a notebook. Each day he reviewed the previous words and received a new list.

Bumsock was very good at math operations. He could add, subtract, divide and multiply and get the right answer the majority of times. But he wasn't able to complete word problems for several months, and then only the simple ones, due to the language barrier.

He learned quickly and started to increase his vocabulary. When I knew it was hard for him to grasp the material, we worked together with his dictionary and the computer translation. I can honestly say that the monumental growth and achievements Bumsock made in 5th grade was one of my greatest joys in teaching. The challenge was in trying to teach Bumsock for short periods of time one on one and effectively teach the other 29 students in the class at the same time!

The growth of Bumsock's learning was beyond amazing, but the greatest reward for me was when he was able to laugh at my jokes! That made the Americanizing of Bumsock complete. I recall one science project in particular. A team of two students each received an egg, one plastic market bag, string, rubber bands, cotton balls, tape, cardboard, a balloon and one additional item of their choice. The egg would be packed in a manner to protect it, so when it was dropped, it would not break.

The first drop was from the top of an 8 foot ladder. If the egg survived, the students made it to the second round which was from the second floor to the ground floor. If their egg remained unbroken, the team advanced to the highest challenge which was from a terrace to the ground.

Some students packed their eggs in the spool of a full roll of toilet paper. Another team packed their egg in a small box surrounded by cotton balls and attached it to a small parachute made from a market bag. Bumsock took an old throw pillow from a couch that his mother no longer wanted, made a slit in the pillow and placed the egg inside. Only three teams survived all 3 height challenges including Bumsock.

As a 6th grade teacher in elementary school, there were frequent visits from ex-students who have gone on to middle or high school. Other times, we would just run into each other somewhere by chance. It's always interesting to see how they have matured and grown and what they are doing now. For instance the time I ran into a student who was attending law school at the University of Washington.

After I retired and was substitute teaching, I ran into a student of mine at school. As I was walking down the hallway, I heard a voice call out, "Mr. Seaman". I turned and immediately recognized a student I had approximately 15 years earlier. It took me a minute to remember her name, Erika. She told me she was a para educator and was also attending a community college to become a teacher. What I heard next actually got me a little teary-eyed. She said she was taking a writing class and the assignment was to write about someone who inspired them during their life. Erika then told me she wrote her essay about me. Moments like this are rare and impactful and bring meaning to your life. Thank you Erika!

One year, a student wrote a poem to me, not part of an assignment, but just a poem to tell me what I meant to her:

Poem About My Teacher

> I bet you've tied a million shoes
> And cried a million tears
> And embraced a million hugs
> As a teacher throughout the years.
>
> I'm happy you're my teacher
> I enjoy each lesson you teach.
> As a role model you inspire me
> To dream, to work and to reach.
>
> With your kindness you get my attention
> Everyday you are planting a seed
> Of curiosity and asking questions
> To know and to grow and succeed.

> You help me fulfill my potential
> I'm thankful for all you have done
> To make me know and grow
> I admire that you're number one.

Writing is one of the hardest subjects to teach, especially poetry. Many students are writing below their grade level. So when a teacher reads something like this poem and it turns out to be about him, it becomes very special. Needless to say it is framed and hangs in my office at home.

As your students graduate from elementary school and move on to middle school, teachers often wonder how they are doing and if your teaching methods have helped them along the way. A few months after I retired, my wife and I were at a friend's open house party. There were two ladies in attendance who were also teachers and taught at the middle school a few blocks from the elementary school in which I taught. We were all introduced by our first names only. Both ladies asked me if my last name was Seaman. I told them yes and asked how they knew.

They both said they taught at Cascade Middle School and when they taught lessons to their students, several of the kids responded that they had already been taught that by their 6th grade teacher, Mr. Seaman. They went on to tell me that these students praised my teaching ability and recalled how much fun they had in my class.

What these two teachers told me that day was very special and meaningful. You don't often get to hear stories about your teaching effectiveness after your students have graduated.

Chapter 22

Some Sad Memories

Teaching has provided me with an amazing second career in my early fifties. It's been filled with fun, smiles, laughter and knowing that I have had a huge impact in helping to shape the minds of pre-teens as I prepare them for life's challenges in the real world. But sometimes, life throws a curve and you encounter setbacks, defeat or tragedies that break your heart.

I had Chez in my first year of teaching 6th grade. His smile was contagious. Students and teachers were drawn to him by his fun and quirky personality. He was smart and asked probing questions. He was definitely the class clown. But he could also be annoying and disruptive, and at times needed reminders to reign it in. There were occasions when he would make me laugh when I was trying to be serious and there were times when he was serious and reflective. He was always respected by his peers.

On November 22nd, I frequently would spend some time talking about the JFK assassination, which happened on that date in 1963. I talked about the conspiracy theories vs. the lone gunman theory which was the subject of a

Congressional investigation. The students were fascinated by all the speculation that the mafia was behind the killing, or Fidel Castro from Cuba, or the CIA. Even vice-President Lyndon Johnson was suspected. I told the class if they wanted to know more about these theories, they should rent Oliver Stone's movie, JFK.

Usually when a book or movie is recommended, the recipient of your suggestion frequently does not follow through. I wasn't sure if any of my students would watch this 2-part video over the weekend.

When we returned to school on Monday, I was curious to find out if there were any takers on my recommendation. When I asked the class if anyone rented the movie, only one hand went up – yes, it was Chez. During the next few days, the two of us had many lively conversations about our favorite theories.

A few months later, I rewarded the class with an extra recess for some outstanding classroom behavior (something I stopped doing a year or two later). When we were outside, I challenged some of the kids to a one-on-one basketball competition. I defeated each one until the championship came down to Chez and myself. We alternated baskets until the next one would determine the winner.

I am very competitive, and knowing that Chez would do everything he could to beat his teacher, I knew I had to resort to whatever strategy could swing the odds in my favor. So as Chez was dribbling the ball at midcourt and planning his game winning shot, I got in his face and started trash talking about his basketball ability. I told him he sucked at basketball, he was going down and I was going to kick the crap out of him.

My words sent shock waves through his entire body. He started laughing so hard, he stopped dribbling and collapsed to the ground. I picked up the ball, slowly walked to the basket and made the game winning easy layup.

After Chez had a chance to regain his senses, he came over to me, and as our eyes met, we both started laughing until our sides hurt. There aren't many students I would have said these words to, but I knew I was safe from any discipline action and I was pretty sure we would be laughing about this for a long time.

About 6 years later, I got a call from Jerry Watson who was Chez's 5th grade teacher. He asked me if I had heard what happened to Chez. Whenever you get a question that starts with, "Have you heard what happened to ……. you know it probably isn't going to be good. Jerry then told me that Chez was in a gang and was shot and killed in a retaliation shooting outside an Arby's in Kent, Washington. It was an incredibly sad day for me. I just couldn't understand why he ended up in a gang, with his loving personality and zest for life. I think of him often with so many wonderful memories, but tainted with so much sadness. His killer was apprehended a short time later and is serving a 39 year sentence.

A few years later, there was a girl who lived just 4-5 houses from the school. Her dad, who was very active in the PTA and other school activities, would walk her to school each day. On this occasion, when he returned to his home, there were 3 boys in their mid-teens running out of his house carrying some of the contents. When he shouted at them, one of them drew a gun and shot and killed him. I later found out that one of the boys (not the shooter) was a foster step brother to one of my students. This was a very rough time for both students and staff and is a reminder of how violence can surround so many young and innocent lives.

One year, I had a student by the name of Blessing. He was the most polite student I ever had. An average student who always gave a good effort. Unfortunately, his mother was someone who interfered inappropriately. She came to school a few times to meet with me, but my answers to her questions did not satisfy her. She brought hundreds of pieces of paper from Blessing's work and quizzed me about each one. Most were problems done on scratch paper, or drafts which were unimportant. It was very embarrassing to Blessing and I could only wonder what his life was like at home.

Seven years later, I heard on the news about 2 young men who broke into a home and grabbed a teenager from his bed, dragging him into the garage. Badly injured, with a leg they attempted to sever, the victim managed to escape and find help. I soon heard the reporter say Blessing's name and I was literally in shock. As this story went forward for several days, I came to find out that Blessing was not sure if he wanted to participate in the attempted murder, but after thinking it over, he joined his friend in the grizzly attack. They were both convicted and sentenced for a 25 year incarceration.

I've had two students come back to see me a few years after they graduated bringing their new born babies with them. I believe they got pregnant when they were 15-16 years old. One even had twins.

It is interesting to note that the school district at that time did not advocate for the 5th and 6th grade teachers to discuss the various types of birth control when teaching sex education. The only thing that was emphasized was abstinence. Statistics show that 400,000 American girls aged 15-19, give birth each year. It took the district several years to alter their stand on bringing birth control into the mix of sex education. I personally discussed this topic with the class even when this information was to be withheld. I never got in trouble, but if I did, it would have been worth it to have a few less mid-teen mothers.

After 10 years of teaching "my way", I had a teacher who was also a good friend come into my room after school and say to me, "Are you aware that another teacher has told several teachers that you teach whatever you want?" I asked her if that meant I wasn't teaching the required curriculum and she replied, "yes, it was strongly implied that you did not follow the required curriculum." She said she thought I should be aware of what was being said behind my back. I asked her if she thought these teachers believed what was being said about me. She said she did not know, but she knew these accusations about me were not true. I thanked her for informing me of this bombshell. When I asked her who was spreading untruths about me, she said she would prefer not to reveal this person's name.

While my teaching style was unique and unorthodox, I always satisfied the required curriculum. I just did it using different techniques which had proven to be more effective than other teaching methods.

When she walked out the door, I was feeling extremely hurt by these comments and did not know what to do. No one likes to be thought of in a negative way by their peers, so I decided to confront some of the other teachers. I was told they were 3rd and 4th grade teachers. Some knew these comments were not true about me and others accepted my explanations. I felt better to know that my talks were received in a positive manner. I found out who had spread this gossip, but chose not to confront her. She transferred to another school the following year, but not before she caused a lot of sadness and frustration in my life.

Chapter 23

Poems to My Students

Starting in my third or fourth year of teaching 6th grade, I wrote a poem to my new students and placed it in the front window of the classroom. Each year, a new poem would appear in the window. Following are a few of my rhymes:

No Escape

Welcome to Mr. Seaman's class.
I hope your summer was fun.
Now it's time to start again
As you enter room 251.

Listen and follow directions
And do your best to shine.
Prepare yourself to learn
'Cause the next nine months you're mine

Jim Seaman

Mr. Seaman's Recipe for Learning

Step into my lab where miracles will take place.
It'll take 180 days after entering my learning place.

I have a magic potion to stimulate your brain.
After one small sip, there'll be no learning pain.

A pinch of listening skills and ideas you'll each share.
A measure of special lessons will get you to really care.

A twist of laughter and silliness and I'll add in lots of fun
And if you each are responsible, you'll all be number one.

I'll toss in some simple rules and respect for each of you.
I'll cut away the bulliness and start to mix my brew

I'll take all of these ingredients and begin to shake and stir.
If you give your best and do the work, then learning will occur.

I'm A Teacher and I Love My Job

Please raise your hand if you want to speak
I've repeated myself each day this week.

Stop walking around and take your seat.
You know the rule, you cannot eat.

Please don't talk, we're taking a test.
No need to become a student pest.

Pick up papers, your floor's a mess
Or stay in to clean it during recess.

You're chewing gum, go spit it out.
I've asked you twice, do I need to shout?

Why are you always late each day?
Set your alarm and be on your way.

You know it's wrong to pass a note.
Should I read to the class what you just wrote?

No time for homework to get done.
Maybe you're having too much fun.

Jim Seaman

Complaints of bullying were on a report.
Do you want to appear in my student court?

"I cut myself, I need a band-aid"
And just when it's quiet, another tirade.

There's days so hard I want to sob,
But no matter what, I love my job!

Perseverance

Never settle for average
When you can be the best.
Never settle for okay
When you can pass the test.
Never settle for ordinary
When there's a treasure chest.
Never settle for second
When you can win the contest.
Never settle for mediocre
When you can reach the crest.

Captain Seaman's Ship of Knowledge

We've been docked awhile for summer,
But the winds of knowledge prevail.
So hop on board, get ready to learn
As we raise the anchor and sail.

The treasure we seek on this voyage
Are not jewels nor coins nor gold,
But all the mental treasures
Your eager minds can hold.

Jim Seaman

The coins you hope to find buried
Are new methods for solving math.
And the treasures of creativity
Will set you on the right path.

The sparkling jewels you're seeking
Aren't buried in the ground.
But in your imagination
Pearls of wisdom may be found

There may be storms along the way,
But we'll navigate with ease,
And if you follow the Captain's lead
The voyage will be a breeze

As we sail into another year,
We'll be fearless, brave and bold.
And when this adventure comes to an end
We'll all be "good as gold".

A Teacher's Job to Educate

We help the kids to concentrate,
We teach them how to punctuate,
We show them how to calculate,
And with our help they'll estimate.

We teach them how to illustrate,
And show them how to hyphenate,
We give them blocks to manipulate,
And help them all communicate.

They watch us as we demonstrate
And listen as we elaborate.
We'll get their brains to activate,
No longer will they hibernate.

When in doubt they'll deliberate,
Then new ideas they'll cultivate.
We'll teach them how to speculate,
Then they will all participate.

Jim Seaman

We want them all to contemplate.
Their minds we want to captivate.
If stuck, we will reiterate.
When they get it, we congratulate.

Our goal is to stimulate
And find a way to motivate.
Then after they all graduate
We'll nod and smile and congratulate.

Give Math a Chance

(Must be recited as a rap poem)

Each year I rapped this poem to my 6th grade class when I was teaching math.

When you want to do the math
Forget the warpath.
Don't become a psychopath
Or jump into a scalding bath.

Just come up with a plan
You know you can.
Don't stand in front of a moving van
Or jump into a frying pan.
Don't run and hide in a trashcan.
Remember that you're not a caveman
Just know that you can
When it comes to math, yes you can.

No need to strain
Just use your brain.
Don't go insane
Or Start to complain.
Don't sell yourself down the drain
Or get blown away by a hurricane.

Jim Seaman

Don't let yourself get a migraine,
But remember no pain, no gain.
So just use your brain
When it comes to math, just use your brain.

Math can be fun
And you're number one
No need to run
Or stare at the sun.
So do the math and get a hole in one.
Do the math and become top gun.
Because you are number one,
When it comes to math, you're number one.

Don't take the wrong turn
Or have heartburn.
Or any concern
And when you sleep don't toss and turn
When it comes to math yearn to learn
Yes you can learn.

Whatever your circumstance
Let's give it a chance.
Your ability in math can advance
Because this poem is a hypnotic trance

So let's get the ants outta your pants
And do the math dance.
Give math a chance
For each of you, just give it a chance.

Jim Seaman

We're All A Star

(I wrote and read this poem to my 6th grade class during their graduation ceremony my last year)

I wonder what life would be as a star
Singing my songs and playing guitar.
Or maybe my own T. V. show
Or hitting home runs as a famous pro.

Filming while traveling all over the globe;
Money no object for my new wardrobe.

Maybe I'll dance as I rap my songs
With cheers and applause from the screaming throngs
Or scripts to learn, long hours to shoot,
Maybe an Oscar as a tribute.

Wherever I go they wait in line
Hoping for autographs I will sign.
Life as a star could really be neat
Exciting, rewarding, a fabulous feat.

But then a thought occurred to me
Perhaps I'm already a VIP.

My Students Taught Me How To Teach

The classroom's my performing stage.
My fans are students, pre-teenage.
The songs are lessons I explain
That give them knowledge they'll retain.

I don't travel the world, it comes to me;
Many of them from across the sea.
The scripts are the books that we all read.
The cast, my students who will succeed.

When the kids understand, it's a job well-done.
When they pass a test, I've hit my home run.

My autographs are the comments I write
When I'm grading papers late into the night.
The Oscar I win is from each classmate
When it's time for them to graduate.

Chapter 24

Some More Crazy Stuff

One day when we were in the computer lab, I noticed a small brown paper bag sitting on the counter. With my curiosity piqued, I opened the bag to discover one diaper. I asked the class if anyone had lost their diaper. After we kidded and laughed a bit, I returned the diaper to its bag, but started to think how I could turn it into a prank in my class.

The next morning when the students entered the room and took their seats, I walked over to my desk and exclaimed, "Oh look, the diaper bag is back!" Again I removed the diaper and made a horrible face as I started to sniff it. I slowly opened it up and cried out ew! ew! When I brought the diaper closer to my face, the kids started to shout and scream. I asked them what was wrong and they pointed to my face and said I had baby poop on my nose. I then turned the diaper so they could see what appeared to be diarrhea and then told the class it looked and smelled like poop, but I wasn't sure. I then took a swipe at the brown stain with my finger and licked it. They were horrified!

I fooled every student, as I continued to lick and eat. When the screaming died down, I told the kids that I had gotten a new diaper that night (needed to make sure it was really clean) and spooned some chocolate sauce into it. The next 20-30 minutes weren't very productive, because the chocolate sauce was still on my nose.

I'm sure no other teacher would do this, and even if they were told about it, they would likely abstain from this and other pranks, because it would take too much valuable teaching time away from the day. But what they don't understand is that I was feeding them the magic formula for improved learning . It's this type of occasional silliness and fun that brings the teacher and students closer in a relationship.and as a result, opens up their minds and expands their learning.

As the school year winds down, most elementary schools have what they call "field day", which is coordinated by the P. E. teacher. Half the school participates in games and activities in the morning while the other half usually watches a movie in their classroom. The students rotate to a new activity every 7-8 minutes when they hear a whistle. After lunch, the kids that were participating in the field events go back to their room and watch a movie and the other kids go on the field. Each teacher is running a specific event.

One year, I was facilitating an activity called "ring toss". There were 2 lines opposite each other with about 8 kids in each line. The lines were approximately 30 feet from each other. Two feet high orange cones were placed in the middle of the two lines. The kids had hula hoops that they tossed in attempts to land over the cone. After about half the allotted time for this event, I decided to change the challenge. I removed the cones, gave my glasses to someone to hold and slowly walked to where the cones had been. The new object of the game was to get the hoop over my body which then became a moving target. There were a few headshots, but the new game was worth the bruises and it was a lot more fun!

Most schools have committee's such as safety, reading, community, etc. and teachers are required to serve on one. They usually meet once a month and it is required that minutes be taken and emailed to the staff. I was on the math committee (each committee has 5-6 members), but when our meeting date rolled around, there were only 2 members in attendance. The decision was to cancel and reschedule our meeting.

A few days later before school started, there were 4 members of our math committee in the copy room. I suggested instead of having our meeting in a room with chairs and desks, we have it in the copy room while one member was using the copy machine, another was using the paper cutter and 2 others were sorting through their mail. The lack of professional setting and multitasking of teachers was well received. I volunteered to take notes. Following is a recap of our unorthodox, yet productive meeting:

The math committee meeting was called to order by Charlene in the copy room with Jim, Evonne and Pam in attendance. Math night was discussed while Charlene was cutting paper, Jim was making copies, Evonne was reading her mail and Pam was looking for colored paper. As the details were sorted out, 2 members needed to go to the library so we all marched down the hallway where we ran into Gus, another committee member. He joined us in finalizing the details for math night. Evonne needed to go to the office, so we all followed along, finalizing the date and time of math night. As I was walking, I continued to take copious notes so we would have accurate information for our staff email. Luckily, no one had to go to the bathroom. I'm not sure what the principal thought, but several teachers told me they loved our meeting format.

Chapter 25

Report Cards

Every teacher's nightmare. Years ago, I divided how teachers reacted to the report card process into 3 groups. The first group were the ones who were ultra-organized, kept up to date on their grading and completed their report cards at least a week before they were due. In other words, the ones we all hated.

The second group, like the first, started in plenty of time, but went at a little slower pace and finished a day or two before the due date. The third group, of which I was the founder and CEO, fell behind in their grading during the trimester. As a result, when the first group was done, this group was still grading papers. There was a 72 hour period where sleep and eating was limited to staying alive and any form of entertainment or relaxation was only a dream.

To be a member of this group, you could not go to bed before 4:00 a.m. the night before report cards went home. After you finished the last card, every member of this group could be heard saying, "I will never procrastinate on report cards again". Unfortunately, we almost never achieved that goal.

Before starting my teaching career, the elementary school report cards utilized the typical A, B, C, D and F grading system. I'm not sure why, but it was changed to 4, 3, 2, and 1 when I came on board. It was assumed there was a correlation between the numbers and letters, but they were slightly different. This number system was accepted by most teachers, but I had a big problem with this. And I felt I had a good reason to question its validity.

A grade of 4 was defined as "consistently doing above grade level work". So when a student achieved scores of 97%, 98%, 99% and many test scores of 100%, the highest grade they could receive on their report card was a 3 +, because a teacher is almost always teaching grade level work. How would you feel if you were an exceptional student, you had your dreams set on getting into college and after getting perfect test scores, you received only B+'s on your report card? It seemed to me this could be quite deflating to one's self-esteem.

I had a student whose mother came to talk to me after she received her daughter's report card. She questioned why her daughter did not get any 4's. She told me she had been keeping track of her scores on tests and they were in the 90-93% range. I told the mother the definition of a grade of 4 (consistently performing above grade level) and her daughter was not quite there. The mother questioned the definition and questioned why it was not possible for a student to get 4's when excelling at grade level. I mention this because the district's policy was confusing to parents and seemed unfair.

If a teacher chose to give that student 4's, it could cause some repercussions on next year's report card. If the new teacher followed the guidelines, that student could receive report card grades of 3+'s. Both the student and parents would certainly conclude that the performance had slipped from the prior year. If a grade of 4 is listed as a possibility, it should be attainable. But when a teacher is doing their job by teaching the required curriculum, by definition, a grade of 4 is not possible.

Because I felt very strongly this was unfair and harmful to the student's self-esteem and because I wanted to reward excellence in special situations, I chose to give deserving students report card grades of 4's. I hoped there would not be problems the following years when their grades might become 3+'s.

To rectify what I thought was a problem, was really a no brainer. Since most teachers used +'s, as a means to elevate a student's performance on the report card. As an example, a student who was not quite performing at the level of a 3, but was better than a 2, could receive a 2+. So why not change the system, where test scores of 95-100% would translate to a 4 on the report card. And if a student is consistently performing above grade level because the teacher is giving higher grade level material, then that student could receive a grade of 4+. The student's self-esteem rises, mom and dad are ecstatic and the teacher knows he did the right thing. Seems like a win-win to me.

In some cultures, report cards are very important to parents. I once had a student who told me if he got anything lower than a 3 on his card, he would be physically punished by his father. So lets' play the pretend game. You are his teacher and this student is at the 2+ level in a few categories in reading and writing. He gets 3+'s and 4's in math. You believe his story when he tells you about his consequences. You are afraid he will be spanked or hit for doing his best. What would you do? After I thought about this, I came up with the perfect solution. I gave him a couple of 3-'s.

While report card grades are necessary, most teachers write extensive comments. No longer is the "*It's a pleasure to have Johnny in my class*" phrase written on report cards.

Teachers take 10-15 minutes per card (and sometimes even longer) to include valuable information to boost the self-esteem of each student and also give suggestions for helping the student improve their grades.

Chapter 26

Yearbook

Taking on the challenge of the yearbook was a love/hate affair. I always enjoyed projects in which I could utilize my photography skills. When I first volunteered it was simpler, since we had not yet started our spirit days and other special occasions which needed to be included in the yearbook. Each teacher was responsible for submitting 2 pages for their class. Eventually, the book included collages of spirit days, assemblies, recess, after school programs, clubs and the individual pictures of every staff member. Special thanks to Vivienne for helping me.

Each year I would set a due date for the teachers to get their pages to me. This way I could send it to the print shop and have it back in time to sell to the student body and staff. There were always slackers who did not seem to understand that the yearbook had to have every class in it and it had to be in the printer's hands by a certain date. One year, I sent the following email to teachers:

"I want to offer some suggestions to those of you who will not have your class pages in the yearbook. When your students ask you why their class is not in the yearbook, some of the following replies might be helpful:"

"Mrs. _____, I asked Mr. Seaman why our class pages aren't in the yearbook and he said you procrastinated. What does procrastinated mean?" "It means that the print shop lost our class page."

"Ms. _____, why is our class page blank?"
"Because I wanted to teach a lesson on visualization."

"Mr. _____, why doesn't our yearbook page have any pictures on it?" "Because I wanted to have an art lesson. Everyone turns to the blank page and does a self portrait. When you are done, pass the yearbook to your right and repeat."
"But what if the principal walks in and we are doing art all day? Won't she get upset?"
"Then I will ask each of you to compute the circumference of your head."
"What does circumference mean?"
"Shut up and draw."

"I hope my email may offer some suggestions to avoid embarrassment when you have to explain your blank pages. Or feel free to use your own."

I was hurt that none of the teachers thanked me for my suggestions. But there were more yearbook pages turned in on time that year.

Another time, I sent the following reminder email to all teachers:

"Many of you use an entry task for math when the students walk in the classroom. I wanted to share the following entry task I had on the board today:"

"Class, as most of you know, I am in charge of the school yearbook. The yearbook pages were due to me yesterday. If there are 25 classroom teachers and 6 have turned in their pages to me, what percent is this?"

"Thai, what is your answer?"
"I got 24%."
"How many of you got 24%?"
"Great job guys!"
"Who would like to tell the class how you got your answer?"

"Yes, Lucy?"

"I wrote the problem as a fraction which would be 6/25. In order to get a denominator of 100, I multiplied 25 by 4. And then I did the same thing to the 6 which gave me 24. I now had a new fraction of 24/100 which would equal 24%."

"Great job Lucy. Thank you."

Can anybody see a message to this yearbook story?"

"Yes, Patricia?"

"Six out of 24 teachers is not very good and if we have to turn in our work on time, I think teachers should have to also."

"Yes Daizah?"

"They are supposed to set the example for us and they are not doing a very good job."

The names, the details and numbers in this email are totally accurate. When I encountered teachers around the school during the next couple of days, I got a lot of smiles and comments like:

"I liked your email", "Thanks for the reminder", but I didn't get all the missing yearbook pages.

My last tactic was a little more serious. I would have the principal talk to them.

Chapter 27

Secret Pal

Each year around February, our school librarian, Trina, headed up a secret pal gift giving event. It was optional, but almost every staff member participated. Each member filled out a form that asked about 25 questions enabling everyone to get preference ideas about the person they would be giving a gift to. Some of the questions were: *If you found $5.00, what would you buy yourself; what is your favorite sweet; what do you need in your class; what is your favorite color; etc.*

Trina's husband pulled the staff member names out of a hat to match them to the person who would be giving them the gift. Gifts were given each day of the week. On Friday, the name of the secret pal was revealed on the white board in the staff lunchroom. The gifts were put in the staff mailboxes or in their rooms if the teachers were not there. In some cases, another person would deliver the gift to the recipient with the comment, "I was asked to deliver this to you by your secret pal".

There was always a lot of guessing around who your secret pal might be, but you were almost always wrong. Some years,

I would deliver my gift to my secret pal and tell them I was asked to deliver this to them hoping to throw them off. I would get a crazy reaction when they found out their secret pal delivered one of their gifts.

The cost of the gifts were to be approximately 5-8 dollars or a total of 20-30 dollars. If possible, I liked to reveal that I was their secret pal in a clever way. One year, my recipient indicated on her form that she collected frames. So on the final day, I gave her a frame with my picture in it – a fun way to reveal her secret pal! Another year, I wrote a poem to my recipient which had clues in the rhyme.

One year, my recipient was Joel. I got a lot of good suggestions of what to give him from the sheet he filled out. He indicated his favorite food was steak, his favorite snack food was potato chips, his favorite drink was Mountain Dew and he liked to give his students decorative pencils. He also said his favorite actress was Jessica Alba. I told my friend Vivienne what I wanted to do and she helped by finding several pictures of Jessica Alba.

As I describe my presentation of gifts to Joel, be prepared they were done with a sexual theme in mind. Beware the following is probably considered x-rated. On Monday, I gave him a steak wrapped in butcher paper with a picture cut out of a magazine of Jessica Alba saying "Eat me". On Tuesday, I gave Joel a 12 pack of Mountain Dew with a picture of Jessica

Alba saying, "Dew me". On Wednesday, he received a large bag of Lays chips with the picture of Jessica covering the s in Lays and my addition of the word "me" added after Lay. On Thursday, I had 30 decorative pencils to give Joel, but I was stuck on how to keep my sexual theme going. I went next door to my buddy Jeff, who knew what I was doing and asked for his help. After he thought about it, he gave me a note which read: "Sharpening instructions: put it in the hole and move it around until it feels just right." I wrapped up the pencils, copied Jeff's instructions on the paper and put Jessica's picture on it. On Friday, I gave Joel a gift certificate to the children's bookstore. On the envelope, I put a picture of Jessica attending a Los Angeles Lakers basketball game. She was sitting next to a man. I cut off his head, replacing it with a picture of my head and a message from Jessica to Joel that read: "Sorry Joel, I like older men."

I gotta say, that was one of my Hall of Fame pranks. It certainly makes for a good story which I have told many times. And again, a special thank you to Jeff for coming through on a difficult challenge.

I also had a lot of fun a few years later, when I drew our office manager's name, Deb Marbet. After she received her 5 gifts, I had another teacher send her an email that requested she come to the school community room where she would find out who her secret pal was.

I planned on using the format from *To Tell The Truth*, a popular game show in the mid 1950's to 1968 as some of you may recall, to reveal her secret pal. There were 3 contestants of which one of them had accomplished something of interest – such as being the real Dr. Seuss. They would stand up and all introduce themselves as the author of Dr. Seuss. The emcee of the show would then read a short description of their fame. A panel consisting of 4 celebrities would each have 2 minutes to ask questions in an attempt to correctly choose the real person, (in this case Dr. Seuss).

I asked Gus to emcee the show and Vivienne and Deb Hodgkin to be the 2 bogus secret pals. When Deb Marbet came into the room, Gus explained she would have to guess the real secret pal by asking them questions. I had prepared Vivienne and Deb H. by giving them a copy of the information sheet Deb Marbet had filled out. I also gave them a list of gifts I gave her and the days they were given.

The 3 of us were standing up as Deb asked questions trying to get enough accurate information from her questions to identify her secret pal. Vivienne and Deb H. did such a good job, Deb Marbet did not guess that I was her secret pal. We all had a lot of fun and the game show provided a great way to reveal her secret pal.

Chapter 28

Walk to Math

Every once in a while, we have a strong feeling coupled with such passion, that we know this is the direction we need to take. Whether in work or play, it is totally obvious this is the only right way. I experienced that feeling with almost everything I did in the classroom. But there was one particular program where the passion was at its highest.

When teaching math in elementary school, especially at the 5th and 6th grade levels, there is a wide disparity in the students' understanding of the material. Usually a little less than half are at their grade level, while there are always several that are 1-2 years behind and a few that are above grade level and need to be challenged. Unless the instructor is teaching a challenge class, this disparity makes it impossible to effectively have every student comprehend how to solve the problems from the lesson. As a result, approximately only 40 to 60% of students in the majority of schools in my district were performing at grade level in math.

This problem was further complicated by the fact that about 30% of 7th grade math frameworks was passed down to the 6th grade. In order for this new material to fit into the curriculum, the 6th grade sent about 40% of its work to 5th grade. This started a chain reaction which culminated in 1st grade sending lessons to kindergarten. Since this work was now being taught at one grade lower, it was difficult for many students to grasp the material.

At the end of the school year (about 5 years before my retirement), the three 6th grade teachers met and discussed having students grouped into their math ability. One teacher would teach the lower spectrum, another the middle group and another the high end students. This walk to-math program was initiated the following year which resulted in an average gain of 4-5% in math scores in all three groups.

We were very excited as we implemented this program for the second year. After several months into the year, one of the 6th grade teachers wanted to stop this walk to math program and go back to having each teacher teach math to their own students. I was very disappointed, but the program was resurrected the following year when a new 6th grade teacher came on board.

During my last two years of teaching, our math scores had terrific gains. In my last year, my middle math group had a student average gain of 18% from 5th grade to 6th grade and 85% of my walk-to-math group was at grade level, one of the highest figures in the district.

This program stopped when I retired. Almost no school in the district has tried it. Math scores are still far below grade level. The three of us who used this method to teach math, are convinced that this is the best formula to narrow the gap between the U. S. and other countries in math. It is at least worth the effort to test this common sense approach in selected schools across the country. Not only does it work, it probably added 5 years to my life from the stress it eliminated.

Chapter 29

Professional Certification (Pro cert.)

I don't know if it was a district or state requirement, but all teachers hired after a certain date were required to complete a program called *Professional Certification* or complete another more intense program called *National Boards*.

The Pro Cert program consisted of choosing a topic about teaching, selecting another teacher or the principal to help guide you during your research and preparing a presentation using classroom experiences relating to the topic chosen.

I dislike doing things that take me away from fun activities or put me behind in my lesson planning or grading papers. And I especially can't maintain a positive attitude about a 50-60 hour project when I am 63 years old and only planning on teaching 4 more years. I attended a few meetings and workshops and then decided I must find a way out.

I went to the district and explained my situation. I was told you have 2 years to complete the program, but after this 2 year period, you can file for a 2 year extension. I quickly did the math and knew if I stuck to my game plan of retiring at age 67, I was home free.

The other option, *National Boards,* is a more comprehensive program that has been created by teachers for teachers and completed by over 100,000 teachers in all 50 states. Research shows that students of Board Certified teachers perform at a higher level. In order to help motivate teachers to complete this program, which generally takes 1-2 years, the Federal Government will pay teachers $5000 per year and the State will pay an additional $5000 per year if the teacher works in a poverty area school.

I feel this annual stipend is a bit excessive. There are schools that have leaky roofs, not enough computers, not enough books or other supplies, no after school programs and most important, not a high enough starting pay to new teachers. As long as these situations prevail, I believe it is morally wrong to offer a stipend in that amount. I also believe if students can benefit from this program, then all teachers should be required to complete this program or a form thereof, after a certain number of years in the classroom. It's not fair that some students might receive a better education simply by having a higher performing teacher than other students.

Most school districts have early release or late start one day per week. The purpose of some of those weekly hours is to improve teaching performance by scheduling workshops and forums for teachers and other staff. Maybe these forms of professional development should be modeled after these *National Boards* where all students can reap the benefits rather than just a few.

There can still be programs offered, such as a Master's degree, in which teachers can receive additional compensation, but $10,000 is a little too much in my mind when so many basic needs are not being met in schools.

Chapter 30

Departmentalization and Looping My Slant: Popular But Wrong

Two programs utilized in elementary school. Both very popular by teachers, but my take, not a good idea. Let's examine the pros and cons of each.

Looping is when the class stays with the teacher for two consecutive years. For example, a 3rd grade teacher would keep their same students for the following school year and teach 4th grade. The advantages, and what made this program popular among principals and teachers, is that the instructor would already know the strengths and weaknesses of each student. This could save several weeks, or even months of acquiring a sense of what makes individual students tick. There is no question that this strategy sounds effective. There are definitely unarguable merits to looping, but you need to understand there is another side.

I believe there are 4 reasons that support the negatives of looping. The first two have to do with the style and effectiveness of the teacher. Teachers are very different. They have different styles and personalities, likes and dislikes and different teaching philosophies. Some may not enjoy teaching science or health or social studies and not offer the students a complete curriculum on what is required. Some may want to challenge their students more. Some may be very tough graders which can impact self-esteem. Some may not form good partnerships with parents. Others may be better when it comes to connecting with students.

There are good teachers and okay teachers. There are great teachers and ineffective teachers. I believe that in the case of an okay teacher and especially in the case of an ineffective teacher, no student should have that teacher for two consecutive years. I feel that is wrong and if I were the parent, I would talk to the principal or the district if necessary to make sure that did not happen. Looping overlooks this potential situation.

The flip side is also important. If a teacher really excels at their craft, then as many students as possible need to share in the special qualities they offer the student. As a parent, I would love to see my son or daughter looped with a great teacher, but I understand there is some selfishness in that thinking. There are not that many extraordinary teachers, but all parents hope their child will experience these special talents.

The third argument against looping, is the need for different student environments. They need to learn how to form new friendships, work effectively in different learning groups and have the opportunity to experience new influences on their behavior and learning modes.

The fourth reason I am opposed to looping, is the need for the teacher to learn the curriculum for two different grades. It takes a teacher 3-4 years to put together an effective and challenging curriculum. And by teaching the same grade every other year, that teacher may require up to 8 years to be efficient in both grades.

Departmentalization is a program in which a teacher in elementary school becomes a specialist in a core subject. It works best when there are 3 instructors teaching the same grade. So if a school has three 5th grade teachers, one would teach reading, one would teach writing and one would teach math. In the case of science, social studies and health, they could each teach all of those remaining subjects or they could also be part of the rotation. This system becomes similar to middle school and high school, where the students walk to different classes.

The advantages of this program is the development of a stronger teaching plan, since the teachers would only have to prepare lessons for a few subjects rather than six or seven. Teachers would be able to utilize their specific teaching strengths in subjects in which they excel. Also, the teacher would have more time to prepare strong lessons, would not have to grade as many subjects and would become a specialist in their curriculum.

Sounds good! But let's examine the other side. For me, the most important thing in educating students is connecting with the child. If you have a strong connection, everything else will quite often fall into place. Not always, but most of the time. This cannot happen if you are teaching 80-85 students every day. This cannot happen if you only teach your students for 1 ½ - 2 hours each day. And this cannot happen if the kids have 3 teachers and are rotating classes. This is a middle school and high school environment. Ten, eleven and twelve year old students need a role model throughout the day. They need someone who can really get to know them personally, their situation at home, their struggles at school and their interaction with other children.

If I were asked to teach under this model when I was teaching 5th and 6th grade classes, I would have changed schools or districts. Being an elementary school teacher requires more preparation for lessons than middle or high school due to the fact teachers must prepare up to 7 different curriculums. For me the extra work was worth knowing I would be spending a whole day interacting with my students.

Chapter 31

The Pencil Incident

I wanted my last year of teaching to be special and memorable. It was a good class and we had lots of fun and laughter. But unfortunately, sometimes life throws a curve in your direction. In my case, it was a pencil that got thrown.

It started when my class was working on a project. Some students were discussing the next steps for this team project and others were working in the pod area outside the classroom. I heard shouting and a loud commotion in the pod and immediately ran out of the classroom, where I observed a girl chasing a boy while screaming at him. The boy ran into the boys bathroom seeking safety, but the girl continued to pursue him into what was definitely an off limits area. I ran into the bathroom, wondering if this was just a playful incident or a serious confrontation.

I pulled them out, told the girl to take a seat back in the classroom. I asked the boy what was going on and he told me he said something to her when kidding around and she took it the wrong way. He also said he was afraid of her and thought the bathroom would be a safe refuge.

I told her that if there was a problem, she should have come to see me and told her under no circumstances should you ever chase a boy into the bathroom. I was very upset and started to write her up and send her to the principal's office. I did not have the appropriate discipline form and instead chose to record this incident on a sheet of regular paper. But then I stopped and decided to look for the required form. I crumpled up the paper and threw it into the waste basket, which was right at the foot of her desk. I was holding my pencil in the same hand and as I released the wadded paper, the pencil slipped out of my hand, landed on her desk, bounced up and hit her just under the eye.

She started to cry and screamed that I threw my pencil at her on purpose because I was mad at her. She ran out of the class and went to the office to call her parents. I knew this incident had the potential to become a serious problem. But I had no idea what was to follow. Several students told me it was obvious I was not throwing the pencil at her and it was an accident. I felt a strong relief knowing there were witnesses who could support that I did not intentionally commit a serious offense.

Right after school was over, I went downstairs to discuss this with my principal. By the time I got there, the girl's parents had already arrived at school and were talking to the principal. When I entered, the mother started yelling at me for throwing the pencil and made it clear that she believed I did it in a purposeful manner. I told the student, her parents and the principal my side of what happened. I told them there were several students who could corroborate the incident. The parents were so angered, they told the principal they were going directly to the district and report what had happened.

At this point, I wasn't sure if there would be an investigation with potential serious consequences or if it would end quickly with no further discussion. Unfortunately, it did not go away. Because the parents chose to file a complaint, the district was required to have an investigation into the incident. I gave a full statement that was recorded. Each student who was in the classroom at the time of the incident was interviewed by a member of the human resource team.

It took several weeks before the district issued their findings. I received a copy of a letter which would be placed in my file. It stated that the pencil throwing was an accident, but it was wrong of me to yell at the student and future yelling could result in more serious consequences. I was happy they listened to my students and relieved the only repercussion was a letter in my file.

After I reread the stern letter, I was curious about the strict warning regarding raising your voice at students. If a teacher could get in trouble for this and have letters of reprimand placed in their personnel file, there could be a serious shortage of teachers. Sometimes we shout or yell in order to be heard. Sometimes we do it because the student needs to know the teacher is really serious.

And sometimes it just slips out in frustration.

So my last year of teaching did have some drama and scary moments, but I was very thankful that the facts from the investigation prevailed and my students went to bat for me.

Chapter 32

My Last Year

When I turned 66 in August, I knew the coming year would be my last. I still had the passion to teach and my love for the kids, but I wanted to enjoy the pleasures of retirement, start a writing career, pursue my hobbies in photography and poetry and not have to set an alarm clock every morning.

I wanted the year to be special, but since I had given my very best to every class, every assignment and every lesson on every day, there wasn't much more I could do. But I wanted to be better and funnier and even crazier in my swan song year. I tried a few new things that were amazing and that I wished I had implemented before. I had some of my best lessons in poetry and writing. The kid's brochures they designed on the computer were the best ever. My math state test scores were some of the highest in the district. We worked hard, we laughed hard and we even partied hard (student birthdays). Teachers came up to me every day and asked about my plans for retirement.

I decided to do something visual and fun. With a month left before my retirement, I asked my wife, an artist, to create a t-shirt with a caricature of myself lying on a hammock stretched between two trees. It depicted me asleep on the hammock with a book lying on my chest – the title of which was "How to Do Nothing". Above the artwork was written: Only 18 days till…. Each day, I crossed out the previous number and counted down day by day. I washed the shirt daily so I could wear it to school every day until I was officially retired at day zero!

On the last day of school, the 6th grade students from all three classes signed their names with comments and well wishes on a 10 foot by 5 foot roll of paper. At the end of the day, there was a school assembly in which awards were given out to deserving students. But before the awards ceremony, the school showed a slide presentation to the kids and staff representing a collection of all the crazy attire I wore on spirit days. The applause and cheers I received were mind blowing. I was asked to say a few words, but was too choked up to speak.

On the Saturday after school ended, the staff threw a dinner party and 'roast' for me. Just because I was being honored didn't mean that I couldn't still have the last laugh. I had thought about what I could do to make a special entrance for my retirement party. When my wife and I slowly entered the banquet room, I was shuffling along on a walker, which I had rented. I had attached a horn to the bar which I tooted as I walked in. The icing on the cake was the bag of Depends diapers sitting in the attached basket which hung under the handle bars.

The first thing I noticed when I went to take my seat were over a dozen of the tiger t-shirts designed by students, hanging on the wall. Many teachers volunteered stories of some of the memorable antics I had done over the years. I was roasted, toasted and presented with some special gifts. Sarah had made a quilt in which the patterns were from several Mt. View tiger t-shirts.

A few months before my retirement, I was visiting with Vincent, the special education teacher, in his room. I commented on how nicely his rustic wooden rocking chair would fit perfectly in my log house. It was handcrafted with wooden slats and willow branches. I had no idea that Vincent had filed that comment away and I would be receiving one from the staff at my retirement party.

To be the recipient of humorous jokes and funny recollections from everyone and enjoy a good hardy, fun filled roast by your colleagues is so amazing. The laughter, speeches and gifts were a special culmination to an extraordinary career. I had a poster in my room for many years which said, "Never settle for the ordinary when you can have the extraordinary". I frequently discussed the importance of those words with my students. And that night I knew an extraordinary time in my life was coming to a bittersweet close.

Chapter 33

Life as a Substitute Teacher

When I retired, I knew I would need to supplement my social security income by subbing. I also knew from the notes that my subs left me when I was teaching, that this was a very stressful job. Many students like to challenge subs. They think because their teacher isn't there, they can get away with unacceptable behavior. I have heard stories about subs walking out of classes, subs being brought to tears and others walking away from teaching altogether.

My classroom style typically allowed for fun and humor. But it is almost impossible to bring those components into the classroom as a sub. Because you are new to them and they probably have not seen that type of teaching, you will rapidly lose control of the class. So, for me, being a sub was very difficult since I could not be myself. Occasionally, there were times when I was in a well behaved class and I was able to loosen up and introduce some fun and levity.

The key to subbing is to pick your comfort zone. For me it was 4th, 5th and 6th grades. To pick up an assignment, you would log into your district's sub-line. There, you would be able to choose the school, the teacher, the grade, the days and if it was a half or full day. For a part time job (for some it was their full time job), there may not be anything quite like it. You can pick the assignment that most appeals to you or just go back to sleep!

The districts vary in pay. In my district, it is a graduated salary. A full day's pay starts at $147. After 20 non-consecutive days, it is raised to $157 and after 40 non-consecutive days it is raised to $162. This breaks down to approximately $21.00 per hour.

When you sub in a class that is well behaved you always want the teacher to have you back to sub again. Sometimes the students will tell their teacher that you were a good sub and they want you to sub for them again. Sometimes, if you leave really thorough notes about the day, the teacher will appreciate your dedication and call you to come back. One favorite thing I did whenever possible was to write copious and relevant notes on the board when teaching a lesson. At the end of the day, when a student asked me if they could erase the board, I would tell them to leave the lesson notes there. I wanted the teacher to see how effective my lesson was. This worked many times as I was asked to come back to some great schools and classes.

One day I had an afternoon only 6th grade assignment. I had been to the school many times before, but not that class.

I did not remember I had subbed for many of the students before when they were in 5th grade and evidently they really liked me. When I walked into the class and they saw me, they started screaming and hollering how happy they were to see me. Some even came up and hugged me. This went on for at least a minute. I looked over at the teacher who had not yet left and she was laughing hysterically. She remarked to me she had never seen anything like that.

I've subbed in schools, where, when I walked down the hallway, there would be dozens of kids running up to greet me with smiles and say, "Hi Mr. Seaman." That really made me feel special and it made the stresses of subbing much more tolerable.

One day, I was subbing in a 5th grade class. Part of the 5th grade curriculum in social studies is American history. I had recently read something that I thought would be of interest to the class, so I decided to take a few minutes and talk about this little known fact.

I asked the class, "Who was the first President of the United States". Some in the class thought I was crazy, but most answered, "George Washington". I replied, " Wrong!" I then went on to tell them to listen carefully, because they would have the opportunity to make some money with what I was going to tell them next. After that, I had the attention of every student in the class. I proceeded to tell them that there are very few people that know this fact about American history:

In 1781 John Hanson from Maryland, was the first man to be elected President. Our country had not yet written the U. S. Constitution, but was governed by The Articles of the Confederation. This document went through many changes and eventually became our Constitution when Washington was elected. George Washington, was the first President of the U. S. under the Constitution, but John Hanson was actually the first President of the U. S., which at that time, was under the Articles of the Confederation.

The Articles stated that the President would only serve for one year. There were 7 other Presidents under the Articles of the Confederation, each also serving one year, so officially George Washington was our ninth President when he was elected in 1788.

I then said to the class: "Now let me tell you how you can make some money. When you go home today, ask your mom or dad the same question I asked you - who was the first President of the U. S.? When they say George Washington, tell them they are wrong and when they insist they are right, ask them if they want to make a bet with you."

I suggested they keep the bet reasonable (not to exceed $20.00), so when they proved their parents wrong, they would actually receive the money.. I then told them they would have to prove that John Hanson was, in fact, the first President. I instructed them to google his name and the internet will substantiate what I had told them.

A few weeks later, I returned to sub in that same class. As soon as the bell rang and the students came in and took their seats, one raised his hand. When I called on him, he told me he had asked his mom about the first President. I was really excited to hear what had happened. He said that it worked perfectly and his mom gave him $20.00. He went on to tell me and the class that when his dad came home from work, he asked the same question, proved him wrong and made another quick $20.00. Another student told us he bet his dad $100.00 and when I asked him if dad paid up, he said, " yes he did". Other students had similar stories to relate, but just not the $100.00 version.

I did this in many other 5th grade classes throughout the district with the same results. I wasn't sure this was something the district would have approved, but only three things mattered to me: That the kids learned something very few people know, they were able to impress their parents and get a little cash and if this was an inappropriate thing to do, I would not get caught.

I even took it a step farther. In some classes, I suggested they ask the same history question to their regular teacher, but instead of betting money, they waged an extra recess or a party if they could prove that Washington was not the first President. I later found out that although teachers did not know the real truth to this question, they suspected something was not kosher and were reluctant to make that bet.

One day I was subbing in a 6th grade challenge class. I had been there many times before and always looked forward to the assignment. On this day, the behavior of the class was only fair and I was getting frustrated and stressed. I had a plan I was going to implement if the kids were disrespectful to each other and/or me. I told the class, "If you don't get your act together, I will do something you definitely do not want me to do".

About a half hour later I repeated the same comment and again a short time after that. I finally said to the class, "Okay, that's it. I gave you enough warnings." I then walked over to the teacher's desk, sat down, picked up the phone and dialed. And this is what the students heard:

"Hello, is this the Highline School District? Could you please connect me to Superintendent Susan Enfield. Thank you Ms. Enfield for taking my call. My name is Jim Seaman, I am a retired 6th grade teacher from the Highline District and I am subbing today for a 6th grade challenge class at Parkside. They have been extremely disrespectful and I have tried everything I know to get them under control, but nothing is working. I was wondering if you had any suggestions for me. No, I haven't tried that. That sounds good. I can't wait. Thank you again for talking to me. I really appreciate you taking the time. Good-bye."

I got up and walked to the front of the class. While I was on the phone, I noticed looks of concern and fear of the unknown on the faces of the students. I stood in front of them with a long pause for effect. I told the class, "You probably want to know what the Superintendent said to me. She said to tell the class: April Fool's Day!" (and yes, it was April Fool's Day and yes the call was faked).

I heard several students say: "You really got us good, Mr.Seaman! The behavior for the rest of the day was pretty good. This prank is number one on my all-time list of classroom pranks, which probably consists of hundreds of antics and jokes.

Chapter 34

Zero Tolerance

Zero Tolerance is a program which was initiated in the 1990's. It basically conveyed a message to the student body of "one strike and you're out". It sometimes results in suspension or expulsion of students who only committed minor infractions. [1] Sometimes the rule violations were so insignificant, the situation could have been ignored or at least solved by the teacher in the room.

The purpose of zero tolerance is to insure the safety of all students in the school. But the harshness of this program was proved to be ineffective and it has been eliminated in many schools. There are, however, some schools and districts that still enforce this ridiculous strategy.

When I was subbing in classrooms in which some students exhibited unacceptable behavior after several warnings, I would write the phrase "zero tolerance" on the board. I informed the kids there would be no more warnings, they'd had plenty, and if anyone was disrespectful, they would be sent to the principal's office. I used this tactic in a few classes, but then abandoned it because of an article I read involving an example that made me sick. I was so affected by this article, I did not want to be associated with the phrase. In part it read:

"A high school sophomore was suspended for violating the school's no-cell phone policy after he took a call from his father, a master sergeant in the U. S. Army who was serving in Iraq at the time." [2]

When I realized the foolishness of this policy, I did some homework to find more examples of zero tolerance in schools: "A 12 year-old New York student was hauled out of school in handcuffs for doodling on her desk with an erasable marker. In Houston, an eighth grader was suspended for wearing rosary beads to school in memory of her grandmother (the school has a zero tolerance policy against the rosary, which the school insists can be interpreted as a sign of gang involvement). Six year-old Cub Scout, Zachary Christie, was sentenced to 45 days in reform school after bringing a camping utensil to school that can serve as a fork, knife or spoon. And inOklahoma, school officials suspended a first grader simply for using his hand to simulate a gun." [2]

I'm sure you're shaking your head in bewilderment and asking yourself if the educational system has completely lost its mind. I became fixated on these eye opening examples that would make a typical parent cringe. Is this really the acceptable policy in our nation's schools? When a student is suspended for several days, or even a few days, not only are they being denied the learning process for those days, but they may never recoup what they missed in certain subjects.

It's obvious our educational system is broken. We rank 17th in the world in overall educational performance. And even worse, we rank 24th in the world in literacy. [3] These statistics are frightening since the U. S. spends more than almost any other country on the cost of educating students. When you also consider the overreactions of principals and school districts, as has been evidenced by the examples in this chapter, I can't imagine the United States gaining much ground.

How about one more unbelievable example for the road?: "While standing in line for the bus in January 2013, a 5-year old girl told two friends that she was going to shoot bubbles at them from her Hello Kitty bubble gun, then go home and shoot herself with bubbles as well. Their conversation was overheard and reported to the Mount Carmel Area Elementary School in Mount Carmel, Pennsylvania, which initially decided to suspend Madison for 10 days for making a "terrorist threat", and ordered that she undergo a psychological evaluation. It was then dropped to a two-day suspension and reclassified as a "threat to harm others". The counselor who evaluated the kindergartener said Madison was a "typical 5-year old in temperament and interest." [4]

[1] *What Are Zero Tolerance Policies in Schools* by E. A. Gjelten http://education-law.lawyers.com/school-law//whats-a-zero-tolerance-policy.html

[2] *Zero Tolerance School Discipline Without Wigle Room* by John Whitehead 2/8/2011 http://www.huffingpost.com/john-w-whitehead/zero-tolerance-policies-schools-b- 819594.html

[3] *Education – Ranking America* Dec. 12, 2012 https://rankingamericawordpress.com/../e

[4] *6 eye-opening examples of zero tolerance discipline* – ABA Journal http://www.abajournal.com/gallery/zerotolerance/999

Chapter 35

Leave No Child Behind

I am including this chapter to inform readers of how inefficient our government has been in its attempts to fix our broken education system. If you're a teacher, you already know this. If you're a parent, you may have some idea that education needs help. Most already know that our Congress recently had an approval rating of less than 10%. Most of the legislation it enacted looked good on paper. "Leave No Child Behind" was created by a bipartisan group of politicians which, in itself, is a rare occurrence.

"Since the No Child Left Behind (NCLB) law took effect in 2002, it has had a sweeping impact on U. S. public school classrooms. It affects what students are taught, the tests they take, the training of their teachers and the way money is spent on education.

Despite rages over whether this law is an effective way to improve academic achievement, Congress was scheduled to make a decision in 2007. But efforts stalled amid criticism of the law from both Democrats and Republicans and arguments over how to change it." [1]

As is true in any controversial topic, there are always two sides. "NCLB advocates say the landmark law holds schools accountable, empowers parents and is helping to close the achievement gap in America's schools." [1]

But "many critics, including those who agree with the law's goals, argue that it is a 'one- size fits all' approach to education that overemphasizes testing and doesn't provide enough money to schools to achieve success." [1]

Parents aren't taking advantage of free tutoring or the opportunity to transfer their children to higher performing schools in the district if their school is not attaining the goals set by the state. The state standardized tests determine if the schools are making "adequate yearly progress" or AYP. If these goals are not met for every student to be proficient in reading and math by 2014, there are severe consequences for the school.

The NCLB law sets up standards for schools to meet. If these standards are not met, the schools face mandatory changes such as tutoring, after school programs and remedial classes. If schools do not meet their AYP goals after 4 consecutive years, staff may be replaced. After five consecutive years, the state can take over the school and it may be converted to a charter school with major staff restructuring. [1]

This is where the NCLB law and the reality of life in the classroom tend to collide. The law is assuming that with extra training and an improved curriculum, the students' work will improve and they will then meet the goals set by the state. Again it sounds attainable and fair.

But what about the students who don't do their homework and as a result, don't understand the lessons. Or students that don't pay attention in class and are unable to "get it"? What about the students who have excessive legitimate absences and have missed a lot of assignments? What about a teacher who misses several weeks, or longer, due to illness and the subs are not qualified enough to move forward? Or the time students miss in class due to the ridiculous suspensions resulting from the insanity of zero tolerance? And up until "Common Core", the scores from Special Education students, whose performance was at least 2 years below grade average, counted on the state tests. In other words, if a 6th grade student was learning 4th grade math, he would be tested on 6th grade math, for which he has never had instruction. His score would count on the state's year end test despite this discrepancy.

Another situation which could have an impact on low test scores, and in turn affect the self esteem of students, is that some principals periodically move teachers from one grade to another even when the teacher is against the change.

All of these situations could easily have a direct impact on a school by making it very difficult to achieve their goals.

Another adverse situation resulting from NCLB is the stress it puts on teachers. Many teachers are focusing only on reading and math, the two subjects which NCLB tests and cutting back on social studies, science, health and art.

"……the Civil Rights Project, formally known as the Harvard Civil Rights Project, concluded in 2006 that NCLB is failing to close the achievement gap, won't make its 2014 goals and has not significantly improved reading and math achievement." [1]

Many states have a serious shortage of teachers, which in many cases, may be blamed on low pay. With this shortage, there are countless classrooms staffed with unqualified teachers.

In the state of Washington, the starting salary for a first year teacher is now $34,048. [3] Most teachers, especially during the first couple of years, are going to work approximately 55 hours per week, if not more. In addition to actual teaching, the planning, grading, researching, copying, meetings, etc account for this. If you do the math for the 180 day school year, you get $189.16 per day or $945.80 per week. But based on the 55 hour week, a first year teacher would make approximately $17.00 per hour.

Statistics show that 40-50% of teachers leave this profession within the first five years. Also 9.5% leave before the end of their first year. This turnover rate is about 4% higher than other professions. [2]

It generally takes 3-5 years for a teacher to become really effective at their craft. Considering the above statistics, almost half of them are gone just as they become efficient, and then the cycle starts all over again.

With this information at hand, we need to ask ourselves these questions; What are the chances our education system can be repaired? Can we really attain goals that are placed on us by the federal government? The number one reality check to reach higher scores, is the number of students in each class, especially in grades K-3. Classroom size should not exceed more than 17-18 students, yet current classroom size can exceed 28-30 students. So another question to ask would be: Where is the money coming from to build more schools, thereby decreasing the number of students in a classroom?

We've been working on fixing our education woes for a very long time, but it seems like we are spinning our wheels or perhaps falling even farther behind.

[1] *What the No Child Left Behind law means for your child* by Great Schools Staff http://www.greatschools.org/gk/author/greatschoolsstaff/ March 8, 2016

[2] *Why do teachers quit?* by Liz Riggs www.theatlantic.com 10/18/2013

[3] *Washington K-12 Salary Allocation Schedule for Certified Instructional Staff* www.k12.wa.us/safs/PUB/PER/salAllocSchedule.pdf

Chapter 36

My Take

I wanted to have the opportunity to share some of my ideas about what could be done or in some cases should be done to help repair our education system. I've always been a free spirit, trying to find better ways to get through to students. I worked within the confines of teaching the required curriculum, but also subscribed to the theory of operating within common sense.

Kids learn better when they have fun, kids learn better when they are engaged in projects, kids learn better when they are grouped by their learning ability, kids learn better when they are challenged and kids learn better when they feel good about themselves. I would estimate this classroom atmosphere is currently happening in less than 10% of classes throughout our nation.

Our school system now operates across the U. S. under a program called Common Core. I would like to take what I have proposed above, call it Common Sense Teaching and incorporate it into Common Core or whatever will be its replacement.

My Take:

In my opinion, the greatest single problem in today's teaching system is the lack of response to a child's low self-esteem. There are so many ways children can acquire low selfesteem. Watching their classmates get A's and B's while they are getting D's and F's. Not understanding the work and just giving up. Being picked last for a competitive event. Never being chosen to read their stories to the class. Getting 3 spelling words correct on a test with 20 words.

Never feeling comfortable enough to raise their hands when the teacher asks a question to the class.

Even worse, giving the wrong answer when the teacher calls on them.

When I was teaching at Mount View, during our early release days on Friday we had meetings and workshops to learn about new teaching techniques in math, reading and writing. But never were we taught effective ways to confront low self-esteem. It was recommended that we stand outside our classroom door and greet the students as they entered the room when school started and again when they left to go home. High-fives, hugs, etc. Teachers give compliments throughout each day, they offer to help kids after school, they recommend after school programs and so many other things that will help to boost self-esteem. But that is not nearly enough.

Teen suicide is at an epidemic rate. "Nearly 1 in 6 high school students has seriously con- sidered suicide, and 1 in 12 has attempted it, according to the semi-annual survey on youth risk behavior published by the Centers for Disease Control and Prevention." In 2011, the teen suicide rate in the U. S. was up from 6.3% in 2009 to 7.8%. [1]

"According to the survey, about 20% of high schoolers said they'd been bullied while in school, and 16% said they'd been cyberbullied through email, chat, instant messaging, social media or texting." [1]

It's imperative that our schools address these problems. Many districts have initiated programs for elementary schools in which the counselor or teacher spends time on a regular basis teaching material on bullying and its effects.

Schools are the best source to meet this problem head on. Not only a "great job!" or a high five by teachers, but a curriculum that can break through the pain and discouragement of low selfesteem and have a positive impact on the frightening rise in teen suicides. There are teaching guidelines along with work books that can improve self-esteem and they must be incorporated into the required teaching guidelines. What's more important? Being able to read and solve math problems at the student's grade level or being able to foster high self-esteem and reduce bullying.

I believe the answer is simple. They are equally important and there is no reason they both can't be addressed.

When I was teaching, the school counselor would visit each classroom for several months and teach a course on how to deal with bullying. This was a good first step, but it never effectively eradicated the bullying.

In my opinion, when a child or teenager takes his or her own life, the person or persons who have bullied them need to realize their part in this tragedy. The responsible parties need more than just a slap on the wrist. We need to mandate some strict consequences for bullying or there will never be an end to it in schools and elsewhere.

I once proposed an idea to my school district that seemed like a great way in which exceptional lessons and projects could be circulated to all teachers in the district, rather than keep them solely in one specific grade at one school. I suggested that each teacher send to the district one or two of what they would deem to be their most effective assignment or project in reading, writing, social studies, science, health and art. The district could then review and collate them into a binder by subject/grade and send a copy to each grade level team at each school. The answer I received was that they did not have the time.

Teachers are overworked, underpaid, stressed, frustrated, do work at home and in some cases, go home to their own children, who need their attention. With the new Common Core curriculum, many teachers feel much of the fun and enjoyment of teaching is now gone from their day. An unhappy and discontented teacher may not be as effective or productive in the classroom.

It should be up to each principal and district to attempt to offset these negative feelings.

Some possible perks could be coupons or certificates from nice restaurants for a "buy one, get one dinner free", free movie tickets, occasional catered meals for meetings, volleyball or softball competition between schools in the district, TGIF after school get togethers, poker nights, jeopardy challenge, game nights, a teacher spelling bee in front of the student body and other spirit boosting events Not everyone would show up for every function, but there would be enough to improve the school comradery and eliminate some of the work stress.

Most districts have 3 specialist classes each week in elementary school. Library once a week and music and PE twice a week. What if music was replaced by an arts program that rotated students every 9 weeks for music, drama, art and computer training.

In high school, there is an elective called life skills. Shouldn't this class be mandatory so it might eliminate several potential setbacks later in life. Wouldn't it be advantageous for teens to learn about the pros and cons of extended warranties. Should I pay the extra $100 in case my stove breaks down during the next 3 years? What do I need to know when I buy my first car? Should I have an earthquake kit and what should I put in it? What about a CPR class every year as part of PE. How do I write a resume and cover letter. Help me with my interviewing skills. School needs to be more than the academics. I believe there is a place for "the practical side" in education.

There is something called 'teaching in the moment'. It is defined as an unplanned question or comment that comes up during a teacher's lesson. It may even be something that is unrelated to what the lesson is about. Many teachers will not address the student's inquisitive mind and answer his question, even if it takes just a few minutes. They are under a lot of pressure to stick to the lesson and not deviate with an off topic discussion.

A good example might be when a student heard Donald Trump talking about not letting any Muslims into the United States. This student might have heard this during the Presidential debates, and when he came back to school, he wanted to find out why they would be excluded.

This is how I would handle this situation:

"Let me just finish this short thought on our current lesson and then we can discuss your question."

I would then answer the question giving what detailed information I knew about the subject and then ask the kids what they thought. Occasionally, I would even have debates if it was a controversial subject. If I was in the middle of teaching something else, there is a good chance I would not come back to it and instead continue that lesson the next day. I might take a half hour or even longer to take advantage of a major current event. I might have the kids write their opinion in class or as homework. These occurrences are not frequent, but if they were, a teacher would have to pick and choose which questions they would respond to. Otherwise, they would fall behind the required curriculum.

I don't know if this is even taught to future teachers while they're pursuing their teaching certificate in college. It was never addressed in school meetings or workshops or offered as a district one day course when I was teaching. To stifle a child's curiosity on a relevant topic for the sake of staying on course is wrong and it goes against the educational process. Yet there is so much emphasis on core subjects and the state test scores, teachers are reluctant to go in the direction of "teachable moments".

My Take:

In 2007, a lawsuit was filed against the state of Washington by an educational network representing two families which claimed the state was not meeting its constitutional duty in providing adequate education to its students.

Washington's Supreme Court set deadlines for the state to comply in providing a plan to increase their funding for education. In 2014 and again in April 2015, the Court granted extensions before imposing penalties. In August of 2015, the State had still not provided a sufficient plan to increase their education funding and, therefore, the Court fined the State of Washington $100,000 per day until they received a plan. As of January 2017, the fines will reach more than $14 million. Not only has the State Legislature not come up with a plan, but they do not know how they will pay the fine. [2]

The McCleary Decision (named after one of the two families who brought the suit) seems to be typical of how our political system works. Since 2014, the members of Washington's Congress have not been able to solve a problem which was mandated by the Court and as a result have gone an additional $14 million in debt.

Maybe this challenge needs to be taken out of the political arena and put into the hands of a non-partisan committee chosen by the Court. How is it possible that a State Congress cannot fulfill its obligation to its citizens in 3 years when this was mandated by the State Supreme Court.

Since the majority of voters were probably unaware of which politicians were sabotaging the efforts to solve this critical problem, I'm sure many of them were voted back into office in November 2016. There needs to be better feedback to voters regarding which elected officials have been negligent in their duties when mandated by the Court. A possible penalty could be enacted in which they cannot run for re-election.

Most schools require all students to read a book of their choice for a minimum of 20 minutes. As a sub, I have noticed that several students in most classes are reading only graphic novels. These are books with few words and comic book type illustrations. In order to improve reading skills, I strongly believe students need to read chapter books or non-fiction. When I was teaching, the students could read graphic novels in class on Friday only or at home. Due to low reading scores, there is great pressure put on schools to raise the students' reading ability. Comic books, although fun for many kids, are not an effective tool to accomplish this.

Many elementary schools have students schedule computer math, usually for 30 minutes, several days each week, in addition to regular textbook lessons. Kids seem to have a greater interest in math when they are solving problems on a computer rather than with pencil and paper. Most computer programs are designed by math strands and when the student achieves a specific score, they move onto a more demanding skill set. Eventually, they move into the next math strand.

One computer program that was adopted in my district for several years was not as efficient as some I observed in other schools. If a student got the wrong answer, the computer did not explain how to get the correct answer. Therefore, the student would keep making the same mistake. I was surprised, with so many different computer math programs available, that this was the one chosen.

When I was teaching, many students struggled in all grades in math. I believe they would give an honest effort the first few weeks of school, but eventually the work started to become more difficult for them to understand and they gave up. The same thing would happen the following year and so on and so on. Maybe the math concepts taught in kindergarten, first grade and second grade is beyond their math comprehension. Maybe math lessons need to be implemented in such a way that the majority of students understand the work. Those students who are working above their grade level can be challenged with more difficult problems. And those who struggle can be recommended for after school programs or homework clubs. If half of students around the country are performing below grade level in math, it seems like the problem may be that the work is above their ability. But the course of action that has been taken has been to have additional training for teachers so they can get through to their students. That may work occasionally, but it will not get math scores up to the 70-80% range.

1 in 12 teens have attempted suicide report by Meghan Neal New York Daily News, June 9, 2012

School funding back on table as court fines state $100,000 a day Seattle Times by Joseph O'Sullivan and Jim Brunner, 8/14/2015

Chapter 36

Conclusion

I have enjoyed sharing many of my teaching experiences, and in some chapters, my opinions about this amazing profession. Its rewards, challenges, frustrations and pitfalls are daily occurrences. As a teacher, I set extremely high standards for myself. I developed a style that was unique, and when the students performed at a higher level, I knew I was on the right track: Have fun, laugh and challenge the students. This formula works! It's a shame this style of teaching is not encouraged by school districts around the country.

I hope this book has entertained you, given you some insight of a school and classroom and most of all, left you with the understanding that, while teachers have various educational teaching styles, we all strive to our fullest to inspire and encourage young minds to grow into big futures.

On my last day of teaching, one of my students, gave me a card with a note inside that read:

"Dear Mr. Seaman,

Thank you for everything. Thank you for making learning fun. You are the best teacher I've ever had. You were so great I can make a brochure of our best times in class. We will miss you. Hope you have the best time of your life after retiring.

From Alex Madrigal"

Thank you Alex for your heartwarming note and best wishes. Alex, I want you to know that I will definitely enjoy my retirement. But I also want you to know that I already had the best years of my life and they were spent in teaching you and the hundreds of other students that came before you.

www.ingramcontent.com/pod-product-compliance
Lightning Source LLC
LaVergne TN
LVHW091538060526
838200LV00036B/661